HISTORIC PALM BEACH

WALKING, BIKING, AND DRIVING TOURS

RUSSELL KELLEY

WITH THE HISTORICAL SOCIETY OF PALM BEACH COUNTY

PALM BEACH, FLORIDA

Pineapple Press

An imprint of The Globe Pequot Publishing Group, Inc.
64 South Main Street
Essex, Connecticut 06426
www.globepequot.com

Distributed by NATIONAL BOOK NETWORK

British Library Cataloguing in Publication Information Available
Library of Congress Cataloging–in–Publication Data
Names: Kelley, Russell, 1949 - author. | Historical Society of Palm
Beach County (Fla.)
Title: Historic Palm Beach : walking, biking, and driving tours / Russell
Kelley with The Historical Society of Palm Beach County.
Description: Palm Beach, Florida : Pineapple Press, [2024] | Includes
bibliographical references. | Summary: "This book introduces three tours
that reveal the history of Palm Beach through its buildings. The tours
are in chronological order and have historical photos from the
Historical Society of Palm Beach County"— Provided by publisher.
Identifiers: LCCN 2024011725 (print) | LCCN 2024011726 (ebook) | ISBN
9781683343721 (paper ; alk. paper) | ISBN 9781683343738 (electronic)
Subjects: LCSH: Palm Beach (Fla.)—Tours. | Palm Beach (Fla.)—Buildings,
structures, etc.—History. | Palm Beach (Fla.)—History. | Historic
buildings—Florida—Palm Beach.
Classification: LCC F317.P2 K44 2024 (print) | LCC F317.P2 (ebook) | DDC
917.59/3204—dc23/eng/20240409
LC record available at https://lccn.loc.gov/2024011725
LC ebook record available at https://lccn.loc.gov/2024011726

CONTENTS

Preface

This book is a companion to *An Illustrated History of Palm Beach—How Palm Beach Evolved over 150 Years from Wilderness to Wonderland* (Pineapple Press, 2020). Much of the material in this book comes from *An Illustrated History* but has been reorganized to fit the tours.

Each of the walking, biking, and driving tours included in this book is intended to introduce a period of the history of Palm Beach as seen through its architecture in generally chronological order. The tours are illustrated with 150 vintage photographs from the archives of the Historical Society of Palm Beach County of the principal structures and vistas included in the tours as they appeared when the structures were first built or how the vistas looked at the time, so the reader can compare them with how they appear today.

Chapter 1 introduces the Pioneer Era (1870s–1894) of Palm Beach with a walking or biking tour that follows the length of Lake Trail from the Royal Park Bridge to the Sailfish Club—a distance of 4 miles. It is the best way to understand the Pioneer Era since Lake Trail was the only real road on the east side of Lake Worth until Henry Flagler arrived and built his two resort hotels and related infrastructure in the mid-1890s. The return route through the North End of Palm Beach introduces the first mansions built on the ocean in the 1910s and 1920s and the grand hotels built on the lake north of today's Royal Poinciana Way in the 1920s.

Chapter 2 introduces the Flagler Era (1894–1913) of Palm Beach with a walking or biking tour that follows a loop around both sides of the Lake Worth Lagoon between the Royal Park Bridge (the Middle Bridge) and the Flagler Memorial Bridge (the North Bridge), where Flagler built his grand hotel and residence on the lake in Palm Beach and laid out the commercial area that became downtown West Palm Beach.

Chapter 3 introduces the boom times of Palm Beach during the 1920s with a walking tour of the midtown business district between Royal Palm Way and Worth Avenue—originally known as the Royal Park Addition—which replaced Main Street of the Flagler Era as the center of Palm Beach.

While the first three chapters focus on the first 60 years of the history of Palm Beach, the more comprehensive driving tour in Chapter 4 covers the town's history from the Flagler Era until today—roughly 100 years of the development of the Town of Palm Beach after its incorporation in 1911. The driving tour goes as far north as the Lake Worth Inlet and as far south as Phipps Ocean Park—a distance of 10 miles, although it can be shortened to 5 miles.

The first three tours are designed to minimize overlaps. The driving tour, on the other hand, which covers the broadest period of the history of Palm Beach, overlaps with the first three tours at several points. To avoid repeating the same history and reproducing the same photographs where there are overlaps, the reader is sometimes given a summary in a sidebar and referred to the chapter with the most complete description and relevant photographs.

Happy exploring in historic Palm Beach!

Russell Kelley
Palm Beach, May 2024

WALKING OR BIKING TOUR OF PALM BEACH DURING THE PIONEER ERA (1870s–1894) WITH RETURN TRIP THROUGH THE NORTH END'S EARLY MANSIONS AND HOTELS

The outbound leg of this tour follows the length of Lake Trail—a distance of 4 miles—and is the best way to understand the Pioneer Era of Palm Beach (1870s-1894) since Lake Trail was the only real road on the east side of Lake Worth until Henry Flagler arrived and built his two resort hotels and related infrastructure in the mid-1890s (see Chapter 2). Today Lake Trail is divided into two sections: South Lake Trail and North Lake Trail, connected by a wide bike lane along Cocoanut Row between the Flagler Museum and Royal Poinciana Way, which is the space formerly occupied by Henry Flagler's giant Royal Poinciana Hotel. South Lake Trail goes north along the lake roughly 1 mile from the Royal Park Bridge next to the Society of the Four Arts building on Royal Palm Way to the Flagler Museum. The bike trail then detours in front of Flagler Museum, cuts east at Whitehall Way, and proceeds north on the west side of Cocoanut Row before cutting back east to the lake on Royal Poinciana Way. After turning north at the lake to go under Flagler Memorial Bridge, North Lake Trail proceeds north a little more than 3 miles to the Sailfish Club.

The outbound leg of this tour can be done either on foot or by bicycle. The return leg goes through the North End of Palm Beach. The first part of the return leg that goes from the end of North Lake Trail nearly 1 mile farther north to the Lake Worth Inlet (sometimes known as Palm Beach Inlet) and then 2 miles south to The Cut at Country Club Road, is recommended for cyclists only since there is no sidewalk or pedestrian trail. The outbound and return legs should each take around 80–100 minutes on foot and 30 minutes by bicycle, without stops. *Walking/biking instructions are in italics.* Commentary is not.

Bicycle Rentals

Bicycles can be rented from the Palm Beach Bicycle Trail Shop located in the Slat House just south of Royal Poinciana Plaza at 50 Cocoanut Row, Suite 117. South Lake Trail starts 1 mile south of the Slat House, at the Royal Park Bridge, next to The Society of the Four Arts building, and North Lake Trail continues 3 miles north of the Slat House, nearly to the Lake Worth Inlet.

Bicycle Rules of the Road

Cyclists under 16 years of age must wear a helmet, but it is recommended that all cyclists wear one.

Bicycles may be ridden both on the road and on the sidewalk.

When on the road, cyclists must ride on the right-most portion of the road and obey the same rules as motorists, including using hand signals to turn and stopping at red lights. When crossing a street, cyclists are encouraged to use crosswalks.

When on the sidewalk, cyclists must yield to pedestrians and give an audible warning when passing pedestrians.

Automobiles must keep at least 3 feet away from cyclists.

Bicycle Rules for Lake Trail

Electric bikes, scooters, and other motorized vehicles are prohibited on Lake Trail.

Cyclists must yield to pedestrians and give an audible warning when passing pedestrians.

Cyclists must observe a 10-mph speed limit.

Cyclists should be careful of pedestrians and cyclists entering Lake Trail from the many narrow lanes on the east side of the trail.

N.B. These rules may change, so check online before setting off.

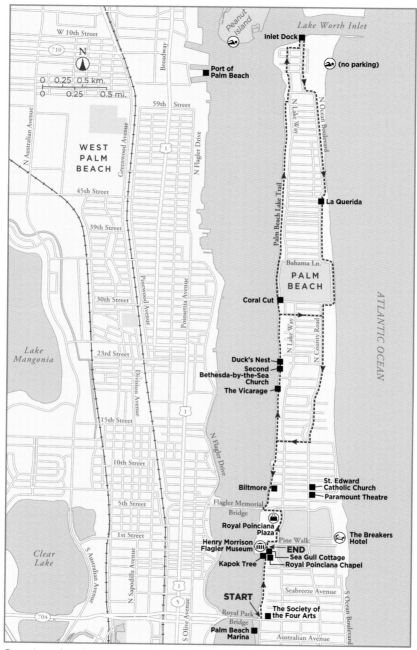

Overview of Walking and Biking Tour of Pioneer Era Palm Beach

Lake Trail to the Sailfish Club: Palm Beach during the Pioneer Era—for Pedestrians and Cyclists

The tour starts at the southernmost end of the Lake Trail, alongside the Lake Worth Lagoon at the bottom of the grass median in front of the Esther B. O'Keeffe Gallery Building of The Society of the Four Arts on Four Arts Plaza, just north of Royal Palm Way. There are metered parking spaces for up to two hours on all streets between Seaview and Hammon Avenues, to be paid using the Park Mobile application (http://us.parkmobile.com). To park for more than two hours, paid parking is available at the Apollo Parking Lot at 405 Hibiscus Avenue just north of Worth Avenue, and at One Parking in The Esplanade at 150 Worth Avenue. Please do not park in the Four Arts parking lots or in spaces reserved for cars with parking permits.

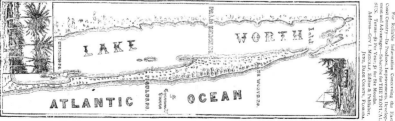

Map of Lake Worth Country on stationery of the Cocoanut Grove House on Lake Trail. The first hotel in Palm Beach operated between 1880 and 1893, when it burned down.

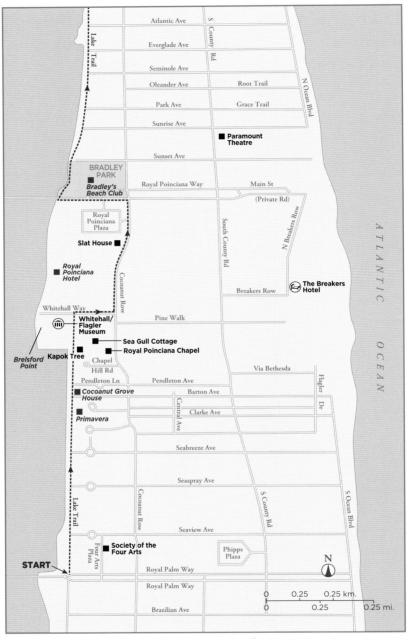

Atlantic Ave

Everglade Ave

S County Rd

Seminole Ave

Oleander Ave   Root Trail

Park Ave   Grace Trail

N Ocean Blvd

Sunrise Ave

■ Paramount
   Theatre

Sunset Ave

BRADLEY
PARK ■

Bradley's
Beach Club

Royal Poinciana Way   Main St

(Private Rd)

Royal
Poinciana
Plaza

Slat House ■

N Breakers Row

Royal
Poinciana ■
Hotel

South County Rd

A T L A N T I C

Cocoanut Row

The Breakers ■
Hotel

Breakers Row

Whitehall Way

O C E A N

Pine Walk

🏛 Whitehall/
   Flagler
   Museum

Sea Gull Cottage ■

Royal Poinciana Chapel ■

Brelsford
Point

Kapok Tree ■

Chapel
Hill Rd

Via Bethesda

Pendleton Ln   Pendleton Ave

Flagler

■ Cocoanut Grove
   House

Barton Ave

Dr

Central Ave

■
Primavera

Clarke Ave

Seabreeze Ave

Seaspray Ave

Lake Trail

Cocoanut Row

S County Rd

S Ocean Blvd

Seaview Ave

■ Society of the
   Four Arts

Four Arts Plaza

Phipps
Plaza

N

START

Royal Palm Way

Royal Palm Way   0   0.25   0.25 km.

Brazilian Ave   0   0.25   0.25 mi.

Detailed maps of the outbound route of Lake Trail/North End tour for pedestrians
and cyclists

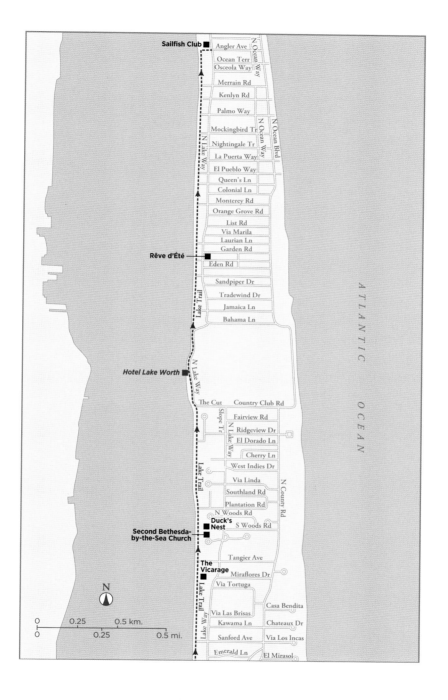

Sailfish Club ■

Angler Ave

Ocean Terr

Osceola Way

Merrain Rd

Kenlyn Rd

Palmo Way

Mockingbird Tr

Nightingale Tr

La Puerta Way

El Pueblo Way

Queen's Ln

Colonial Ln

Monterey Rd

Orange Grove Rd

List Rd

Via Marila

Laurian Ln

Garden Rd

Rêve d'Été ■

Eden Rd

Sandpiper Dr

Tradewind Dr

Jamaica Ln

Bahama Ln

Hotel Lake Worth ■

N Lake Way

Lake Trail

The Cut   Country Club Rd

Fairview Rd

Slope Tr

Ridgeview Dr

N Lake Way

El Dorado Ln

Cherry Ln

West Indies Dr

Via Linda

Southland Rd

N County Rd

Plantation Rd

N Woods Rd

Duck's
Nest ■

S Woods Rd

Second Bethesda-
by-the-Sea Church ■

The
Vicarage ■

Tangier Ave

Miraflores Dr

Via Tortuga

Via Las Brisas

Casa Bendita

Kawama Ln

Chateaux Dr

Sanford Ave

Via Los Incas

Emerald Ln

El Mirasol

N Ocean Way

N Ocean Way

N Ocean Blvd

N Lake Way

Lake Trail

Lake Trail

Lake Trail Way

ATLANTIC OCEAN

N

0   0.25   0.5 km.

0   0.25   0.5 mi.

Walk or bike north for approximately three-quarters of a mile along South Lake Trail past the marker showing where Cocoanut Grove House was located at the intersection with Pendleton Lane. One hundred yards farther north, the pedestrian/bike path makes a detour around Whitehall, where the Flagler Museum is located, where you must jog first right just after the giant kapok tree, then left at Sea Gull Cottage, proceeding in front of the Flagler Museum. (The pedestrian and bike path returns to the lake at Flagler Memorial Bridge. North Lake Trail begins in Bradley Park on the north side of Flagler Memorial Bridge.)

When the first pioneers came to the "Lake Worth Country," as the area around the lake was known, in the 1870s, they all built their houses on the lake, not the ocean, and the Lake Trail was the first road on what became Palm Beach.

In 1876 Elisha Newton "Cap" Dimick and his wife Ella, his brother Frank and his wife Anna, their sister Marion and her husband Albert Geer (the three Dimick siblings had married three Geer siblings), and their parents moved to Lake Worth Country from Constantine, Michigan. All three couples settled in adjacent properties on the lake at the widest and driest part of what became the island of Palm Beach.

Lake Trail looking north, with Brelsford Point in the distance

The Cocoanut Grove House on Lake Trail

In 1880 Cap and Ella added eight rooms to their house to accommodate visitors and opened the first hotel on Lake Worth, and the first hotel between Titusville and Key West. The hotel was gradually enlarged to 50 rooms. They named the hotel the **Cocoanut Grove House** (using the old-fashioned spelling of "coconut") since it was located next to the grove of coconut palm trees that had been

A coconut grove

Brelsford Point, as seen from the Dimick dock in front of Cocoanut Grove House

Croton Cottage was the finest house in Lake Worth Country when it was built in 1886.

Lake Trail in 1900, during the Flagler Era

planted by the settlers in 1878 when the Spanish frigate *Providencia* ran aground south of today's Bath & Tennis Club with its cargo of 20,000 coconuts.

In 1880 Edward and John Brelsford purchased Bonefish Point from Frank Dimick, which thereafter was known as **Brelsford Point,** and opened a General Store. The point protrudes into the lake around 200 yards north of where the Cocoanut Grove House stood. In 1887 the Brelsford brothers opened the "Palm Beach Post Office," in reference to the palm trees that had been planted nine years earlier. In a few years, Palm Beach replaced Lake Worth as the name for the entire lake country.

In 1886 Denver businessman Robert R. McCormick bought Albert Geer's land next to Albert's sister Ella and brother-in-law Cap Dimick's Cocoanut Grove House and built Croton Cottage on the property.

To discover the dramatic impact that the Flagler Era, which followed the Pioneer Era, had on this section of the Lake Trail between the Royal Park Bridge and the Flagler Memorial Bridge, together with vintage photographs, please refer to the first section of the walking or biking tour in Chapter 2, which is summarized in the sidebar below.

During the Flagler Era

In 1892 Henry Morrison Flagler made his first visit to Lake Worth and stayed at the Cocoanut Grove House. He resolved to extend his railroad, which began in Jacksonville, to Lake Worth and to make Palm Beach a resort for the well-to-do.

In chronological order, Flagler bought Croton Cottage and set about building the Royal Poinciana Hotel on the lake, The Breakers on the ocean, and his residence Whitehall (now the Flagler Museum) south of the Royal Poinciana Hotel. He built a railroad bridge, first on the south side of the Royal Poinciana Hotel and then moved it to the north side, so that his guests could travel by rail—often in private railroad cars—from the Florida East Coast Railway's depot in West Palm Beach to their hotels. Next to the train tracks and train station in Palm Beach was Main Street, the center of town.

After passing in front of the Flagler Museum, continue across Whitehall Way, turn right onto the wide, paved path on the sidewalk on the far side of the street that is the continuation of the pedestrian and bike path, and then turn left at the corner and proceed north on the west side of Cocoanut Row.

Continue north past Palm Beach Towers, the Slat House (where the Palm Beach Bicycle Trail Shop is located), and Royal Poinciana Plaza, to Royal Poinciana Way.

At Royal Poinciana Way turn left on the sidewalk. After 100 yards, there is a fork where the sidewalk climbs to the right to go over the Flagler Memorial Bridge and the path descends to the left to go down to the lake.

Take the left fork to the lake, turn right at the lake, and follow the path under the bridge (be careful at the blind turns on either side of the bridge) to Bradley Park, where North Lake Trail picks up alongside the lake.

Continue north along North Lake Trail for approximately 1 mile until you get to the marker for the second Bethesda-by-the-Sea Church.

In 1886 the first schoolhouse in southeast Florida was built near the future location of the second Bethesda-by-the-Sea Church. In 1960 the building, now known as **"the Little Red Schoolhouse,"** was relocated to Phipps Ocean Park in the South End of Palm Beach.

The first schoolhouse on Lake Trail

The second Bethesda-by-the-Sea Church on Lake Trail

The first Church of Bethesda-by-the-Sea was built in 1889 and seated 100 people. It was named by the vicar's wife after the Bethesda church that her family used to attend in Saratoga Springs, New York. In 1895, when the congregation outgrew the first building, a **second Church of Bethesda-by-the-Sea** was constructed on Lake Trail. It was deconsecrated when the current Bethesda-by-the-Sea was built on South County Road in 1927 and is now a private residence.

Duck's Nest on Lake Trail, next to the second Bethesda-by-the-Sea Church

Lake Trail in 1906

Just north of the second Church of Bethesda-by-the-Sea is **Duck's Nest**, built in 1891 by pioneers Henry and Jeanie Elizabeth Smith Maddock of Staffordshire, England. It was originally a modest one-story dwelling made from two portable frame houses shipped from Long Island by Henry Maddock but was significantly expanded in the 1920s, 40s, and 50s. Duck's Nest is the second oldest residence in Palm Beach (after Sea Gull Cottage, which was originally called Croton Cottage). The Maddock family owned the house until 2018. The new owners beautifully restored the house, winning the 2021 Ballinger Award from the Preservation Foundation of Palm Beach, which commemorates the restoration of a landmarked estate that best exemplifies the traditions of Palm Beach's original houses and celebrates the architects who designed them.

Continue north along North Lake Trail to Country Club Road, also known as "The Cut."

The Coral Cut was excavated in the 1920s to provide additional access to the North End of the Island. It was later widened.

Just past The Cut is the golf course of the Palm Beach Country Club. In 1888 early pioneer Harlan Page Dye built the 63-room **Hotel Lake Worth** near here. It was the second hotel in Palm Beach after

the Cocoanut Grove House and the first structure that was designed and built as a hotel in Lake Worth Country, as the area around the lake was then known. After the hotel burned down in 1897, Dye used the land for a dairy farm. In 1913 he sold the land to the East Coast Hotel Company (owner of the Royal Poinciana Hotel and The Breakers), who built a Donald Ross–designed golf course on it, opening the **Palm Beach Country Club** in 1917. It was sold first in 1942, and then in 1952, and the current Palm Beach Country Club was established in 1953.

The Cut

A shooting competition at the Florida Gun Club in 1903

In 1903 the **Florida Gun Club** was established on the lakefront 2 miles north of the Royal Poinciana Hotel. Guests of the hotel could travel by boat up Lake Worth or by wheelchair along Lake Trail. In 1917 the Florida Gun Club property became part of the Palm Beach Country Club.

The seawall along Rêve d'Été

Exotic plants at the Cragin estate

Around a quarter-mile beyond the golf course is a sign on the right for Eden/Garden Roads. This is the site where Charles and Frances Cragin of Philadelphia purchased 20 acres in 1887 and built their house **Rêve d'Été (Summer Dream)**. They added 15 more acres and planted an exotic botanical garden known as the Garden of Eden, which became a popular destination for tourists.

After Frances Cragin's death in 1931, the Garden of Eden was sold to a developer who subdivided the property, creating Garden, Eden, and Adam Roads.

Continue 1 mile farther north from the sign for Garden/Eden Roads to where North Lake Trail ends at the Sailfish Club. First turn right and then turn left onto North Lake Way and proceed north in front of the Sailfish Club.

The Sailfish Club was founded in 1914, making it the oldest continuously operating private club in Palm Beach. Its members first met at

The Sailfish Club, 1948

A remote stretch of Lake Trail in 1898

The Breakers Casino. The club moved to a new clubhouse and dock on its present site on Lake Worth in 1934. The Sailfish Club purchased adjacent land over time and the clubhouse was completely rebuilt in the 1980s. The docks were replaced after damage caused by hurricanes in 2004 and 2005.

This is the end of the 4-mile walking and biking tour of the Pioneer Era. Cyclists may continue for nearly 1 mile farther to the north to arrive at the Lake Worth Inlet at the northern tip of Palm Beach. This area is known as the North End, which began to be developed in the 1930s.

Since there are no sidewalks between the Sailfish Club and Lake Worth Inlet (which is nearly a mile farther north) and for the 2 miles returning south from Lake Worth Inlet to The Cut at Country Club Road, it is recommended that pedestrians turn around here and proceed south as described below. Cyclists can continue to the Lake Worth Inlet as described further below.

Return Route for Pedestrians along Lake Trail to Hi Mount Road

 Turn around at the Sailfish Club and retrace your route on North Lake Trail past the Palm Beach Country Club's golf course to the first lane on the left after The Cut, which is signposted Hi Mount Road. Walk to the top of the steep lane and turn left onto Hi Mount Road.

At 26 feet above sea level, Hi Mount Road is the highest point in Palm Beach.

Turn right on Ridgeview Drive and walk downhill to North Lake Way. Cross North Lake Way and continue east to the end of Ridgeview Drive where it intersects with North County Road. It is at this point that pedestrians rejoin the return route for cyclists (see Route from The Cut Back to the Flagler Museum below).

Pedestrians should turn right on North County Road and walk south along the wide pedestrian and bike path on the west side of the road for 1 mile to Wells Road. Be careful of cars entering the path from streets on the right.

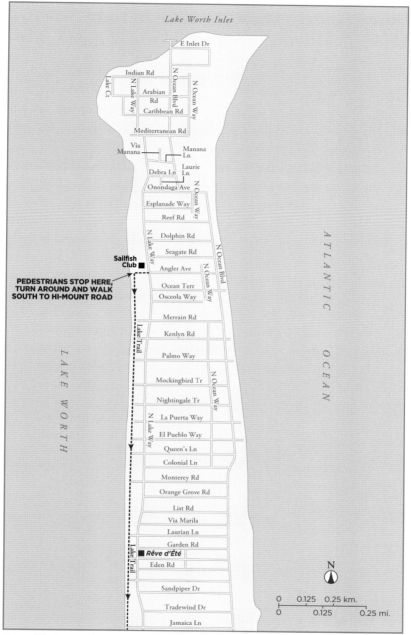

Map of first part of return route for pedestrians (second part is on page 29).

Route from the Sailfish Club to Lake Worth Inlet, and Return Route to The Cut, for Cyclists

This route is not recommended for pedestrians since there are no sidewalks when heading north from the Sailfish Club to the Lake Worth Inlet, or when heading south from the Lake Worth Inlet to Country Club Road.

When North Lake Trail ends at the Sailfish Club, turn right on the narrow lane and bike to North Lake Way.

Turn left on North Lake Way and continue north until it ends at Indian Road. Turn right at Indian Road and then turn left at the first corner onto North Ocean Boulevard and continue 2 blocks farther north until you arrive at the dock at the Lake Worth Inlet. Park your bike in the area next to the dock and walk to the end of the dock.

This is the northernmost point of the island of Palm Beach. When facing north, the Lake Worth Inlet is at 3 o'clock on your right; the Town of Palm Beach Shores at the southern tip of Singer

Looking west, with the north end of Palm Beach on the left, the newly dredged Lake Worth Inlet on the right, the spoil site (Inlet Island, later renamed Peanut Island) on the upper right, and the Port of Palm Beach at the top center

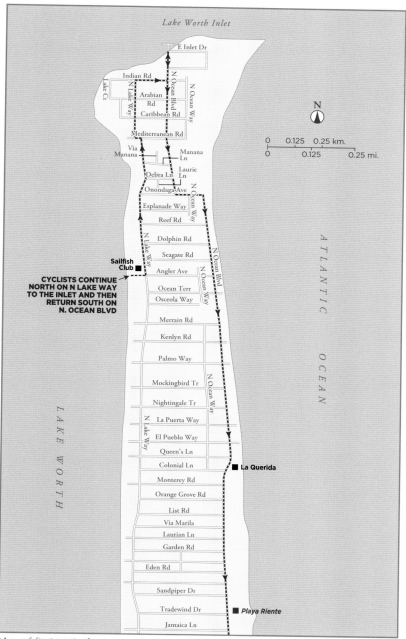

Map of first part of return route for cyclists

Island is at 1 o'clock; the Sailfish Marina in Palm Beach Shores is at 12 o'clock, with the Blue Heron Bridge between Riviera Beach and Singer Island behind; Peanut Island is at 11 o'clock; and the Port of Palm Beach in Riviera Beach on the west shore of Lake Worth Lagoon is at 9 o'clock.

In 1918 the new **Lake Worth Inlet** opened, separating Palm Beach from Singer Island (which Paris Singer started to develop in 1925 before falling victim to the Florida real estate bust of 1927). The jetties were added in 1935, and the channel has been enlarged and deepened three times. Dredging the inlet led to the creation of Inlet Island as a "spoil site," which grew every time the inlet was dredged; it started at 10 acres and is now up to 86 acres. Inlet Island was renamed **Peanut Island** after it was leased for use as a peanut oil–shipping terminal, which failed in 1946. The historic Coast Guard station was constructed on the island in 1936. A fallout shelter was built on the island in 1961 for then-president John F. Kennedy, who frequently visited his family's compound in Palm Beach. Peanut Island is visible to the west.

A wooden dock once stood at the north end of Palm Beach at Lake Worth Inlet. Between 1946 and 1985 it was known as **"Annie's Dock"** after Anne Eggleston, who was the dock master and lived in a tiny house on the dock. The dock had a fuel pump and a bait shop. It was replaced by today's concrete dock.

After leaving the dock, bike straight ahead (south) along North Ocean Boulevard for approximately 2 miles, until the second time the road turns left to go to the ocean and then right alongside the ocean on the left and the golf course of the Palm Beach Country Club on the right, then sharply right after the clubhouse of the Palm Beach Country Club, and finally sharply left at Country Club Road (which leads to The Cut) to become North County Road.

This leg is also included in the Driving Tour of Historic Palm Beach in Chapter 4, but in the opposite direction, from south to north, and with vintage photographs. It is summarized in the sidebar below.

North End Mansions of the 1910s and 1920s

Between 1912 and 1916 **Ocean Boulevard** was constructed between Lake Worth Inlet and Delray Beach. It ran along the ocean bluff for nearly its entire 23-mile length. A half-mile section was moved inland to North County Road after the 1928 hurricane, as described below.

The first 1.5 miles south of the inlet were largely undeveloped until the 1930s, when most of the streets were laid out. After seven streets, North Ocean Boulevard curves to the left (east) at Onondaga Avenue where it then goes along the ocean for approximately 0.8 mile before it turns inland again just after Queens Lane. This is one of the best stretches where cyclists can appreciate a nearly uninterrupted view of the beach and ocean.

The house numbers on North Ocean Boulevard and North County Road go in descending order since the dividing line of north and south in Palm Beach is at The Breakers Hotel.

The northernmost of the great estates built in the 1920s was **La Querida (Dear One)** at 1095 North Ocean Boulevard, which was designed by Addison Mizner for Rodman

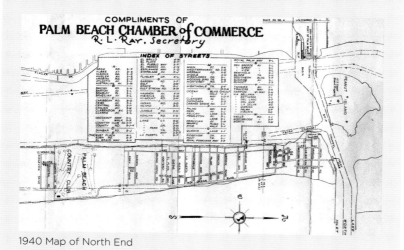

1940 Map of North End

Wanamaker II, who sold it to Joseph P. Kennedy in 1933. After an extensive restoration of La Querida by the previous owners in 2017, the new owners started an even more ambitious expansion in 2022. All that remains of the original structure are the wall and door along North Ocean Boulevard.

Five blocks farther south on the right is Garden Road followed by Eden Road. Starting in 1887 Charles and Frances Cragin of Philadelphia purchased 35 acres where they built their home **Rêve d'Été (Summer Dream)** and planted an exotic botanical garden known as the "Garden of Eden," as described above.

Soon after Eden Road, at 947 North Ocean Boulevard, just before North Ocean Boulevard turns east back to the ocean, once stood **Playa Riente (Laughing Beach)**, built by Addison Mizner in 1923 for Oklahoma oilman Joshua Cosden and later owned by Anna Thompson Dodge. With 70 rooms built on 27 acres of ocean-to-lake property, Playa Riente was Mizner's largest and most elaborately decorated residence in Palm Beach. The house was demolished, and the land was subdivided in 1957.

Once North Ocean Boulevard curves back alongside the ocean, on your right is the golf course and clubhouse of the **Palm Beach Country Club**, 760 North Ocean Boulevard. This is another stretch where cyclists can appreciate a rare, uninterrupted view of the ocean.

In 1917 the East Coast Hotel Company (owner of the Royal Poinciana Hotel and The Breakers) opened the Palm Beach Country Club, the second golf course in Palm Beach, on the highest and hilliest part of the island, on the advice of its designer Donald Ross. The land previously belonged to the **Florida Gun Club**, which was a popular destination for hotel guests during the Flagler Era. In 1952 the Palm Beach Country Club was sold to an investment group which built a new clubhouse and reopened to new members in 1953.

After the Palm Beach Country Club, follow North Ocean Boulevard to the right (west) on Country Club Road and then immediately to the left (south) on North County Road. At North County Road either bike on the pedestrian and bike path on the west side of the road (where the speed limit is 10 mph) or bike on the shoulder of the wide North County Road for approximately 1 mile until you reach Wells Road. On the pedestrian and bike path, be careful of cars entering the path from the roads on the right.

On the left immediately after the curve, at 755 North County Road, is the **Beach Club**, which was built in 1970 on the former site of the **Coral Beach Club**, which opened in 1947 and was owned by Jack Mitchell until his death in 1969. Jack was famous for his colorful attire, wide-brimmed straw hats, and pink Cadillac convertible. Both clubs were designed by John Volk.

From The Cut Back to the Flagler Museum for Pedestrians and Cyclists: Palm Beach in the 1910s and 1920s

 The final return leg below describes Palm Beach between Country Club Road/The Cut and Royal Poinciana Way after the Flagler Era (see Chapter 2), when the first mansions were built on the ocean before World War I and then by Mizner during the 1920s, when more great hotels went up on the lake and iconic buildings were built north of Main Street on North County Road.

This leg is also included in the Driving Tour of Historic Palm Beach in Chapter 4, but in the opposite direction, from south to north, and with vintage photographs. It is summarized below.

Ocean Boulevard before the Hurricane of 1928

The half-mile stretch of Ocean Boulevard between Country Club Road next to the Palm Beach Country Club and Wells Road became known as **"Millionaires Mile"** following the construction of some of Palm Beach's earliest and grandest ocean-to-lake estates. Many of the estates were built on the 1,000 feet of oceanfront north of Wells Road purchased in 1912 by Henry S. Phipps (1839–1930), who made his fortune as Andrew Carnegie's partner in U.S. Steel. Phipps subdivided the land into three parcels where his sons Henry Carnegie and John S. "Jay" and daughter Amy built houses, and sold some of the land to brothers Charles and Gurnee Munn who also built houses.

From their construction until the 1928 hurricane, Ocean Boulevard separated these great estates from the beach. After the hurricane destroyed the road, the landowners in this section successfully petitioned the town to abandon this stretch of Ocean Boulevard, and instead extend

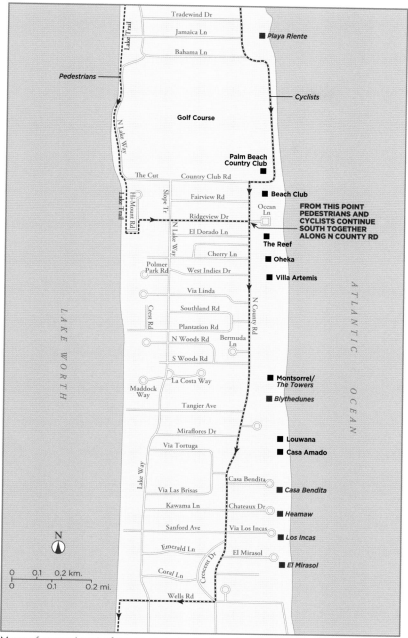

Maps of second part of return route for both pedestrians and cyclists

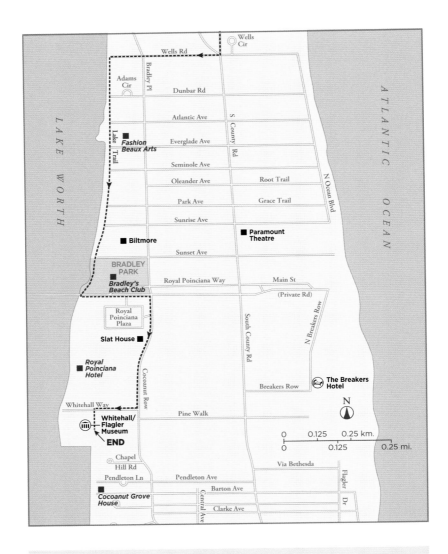

County Road (formerly known as Palm Beach Avenue) north from Wells Road to the Palm Beach Country Club. The estates then moved their entrances to County Road, where they were given the street addresses that are referred to below.

Generally, development started around Flagler's hotels and spread north to Millionaires Mile (and south to the Estate

Section) from there, so you will be seeing increasingly older houses—or their former sites—as you proceed south.

Just south of the Beach Club are two oceanfront houses that were designed by the celebrated architect Maurice Fatio in the 1930s:

The Reef, 702 North County Road, was built in 1935. It is one of the few houses in Palm Beach designed in the International Style.

Oheka, 691 North County Road, was built in 1930 for banker Otto Hermann Kahn. (The name was derived from the first letter of his first name and the second letters of his middle and last names.) After Kahn's death, the estate was sold to the Graham-Eckes School, which occupied the premises between 1941 and 1989. The school then sold the house to an individual owner who converted the building into a private residence once again.

Continuing south on North County Road, the first great estates built on the ocean on Millionaires Mile, and their fates, were as follows:

Villa Artemis, 656 North County Road, was designed in 1916 by Francis Burrall Hoffman Jr. for Henry S. Phipps's daughter Amy Phipps Guest (Mrs. Frederick Guest). In 1967 new owners removed the second story of the house and fundamentally changed the original design of the house. Villa Artemis is still a private residence.

The Towers, 548 North County Road, was designed by Addison Mizner in 1923 for William M. Wood. Two towers, one five stories high, gave the house its name. The Towers was razed in 1965 and Montsorrel (Mountain of Sorrow) was built in its place in 1969. Montsorrel was designed by French architect Jacques Regnault. The guest house across North County Road was built around 1990. The two properties total 13 acres.

Blythedunes, 515 North County Road, was designed by Harold Hastings Mundy for Robert Dun Douglass in 1915. It was demolished in 1985 and the land was subdivided.

Casa Amado and **Louwana**, which share a driveway at 455 North County Road, were designed by Addison Mizner in 1919 for brothers Charles and Gurnee Munn. Louwana was named after Gurnee's wife, Mary Louise Wanamaker. Both houses are still private residences.

Now you will come to the impressive canopy of ficus trees that overhang North County Road.

Casa Bendita was designed by Addison Mizner on 28 acres for John S. "Jay" Phipps and his wife Margarita "Dita" Grace, after whom the house was named. In 1961 Casa Bendita was demolished and the land east of County Road became a 12-lot subdivision. In 1993, 14 acres of the 20-acre parcel on the west side of County Road was platted as the Phipps Estates subdivision. The name of the street Casa Bendita is all that remains of the original estate.

El Mirasol (the Sunflower), 348 North County Road, was Addison Mizner's first Palm Beach mansion following the construction of the Everglades Club with its distinctive Mediterranean Revival design. The ocean-to-lake estate was built in 1919 on 42 acres north of Wells Road for Edward and Eva Stotesbury. In 1958 El Mirasol was razed. After its entrance was moved from Ocean Boulevard to County Road, in the 1930s Maurice Fatio designed a grand new entrance portal for El Mirasol, now at 365 North County Road between today's El Mirasol and Via Los Incas. In 1964 Robert Gottfried developed 12 oceanfront acres as El Mirasol Estates. Maurice Fatio's portal is all that remains of the estate today.

Los Incas was built on 6 acres around 1916 for Michael P. Grace, John S. Phipps's father-in-law, by an unknown architect. It was demolished in 1978 and subdivided; it is now the site of Via Los Incas.

Heamaw was designed in 1916 by Francis Burrall Hoffman Jr., the architect of James Deering's estate Vizcaya in Miami, for Henry Carnegie Phipps. Heamaw was razed in 1972 after the death of his widow, Gladys Mills Phipps.

Just after the ficus canopy ends on North County Road, turn right on Wells Road. Go two blocks west until you come to Lake Trail. Turn left on Lake Trail and proceed south to the Flagler Memorial Bridge.

The Palm Beach Hotel on North Lake Trail opened in 1902 and burned down in 1925.

The stretch of Lake Trail between Wells Road and Bradley Park was once lined with great hotels and commercial buildings like the 400-room **Palm Beach Hotel**, which opened in 1902 and burned down in 1925; the **Royal Danieli**, which opened in 1924 and was renamed the **Mayflower Hotel** in 1930; and the **Fashion Beaux Arts Building**, which was designed by August Geiger in 1917 and was Palm Beach's first stand-alone commercial and entertainment center, with retail stores and a movie house.

The Mayflower Hotel and the Fashion Beaux Arts Building were demolished and replaced by townhouses and condominiums.

The Palm Beach Hotel was replaced by the 12-story **Alba Hotel**, which opened in 1926. The Alba became the **Ambassador Hotel** in 1929 and the **Biltmore Hotel** in 1934. The building was converted to

The Alba Hotel under construction in 1925. It is now the Palm Beach Biltmore Condominium.

A 1930s aerial of Sunrise Avenue with the new Palm Beach Hotel and St. Edward Catholic Church at the corner of North County Road (both completed in 1926) on the left side of the street

condominiums (with 128 units) in 1981.

Follow the trail under Flagler Memorial Bridge, taking care at the two blind corners, then continue on the path alongside Royal Poinciana Way to Cocoanut Row. Turn right on the paved pedestrian and bike path alongside Cocoanut Row and continue past the Royal Poinciana Plaza and the Palm Beach Towers. Turn right at Whitehall Way and then turn left in front of the Flagler Museum, where this tour ends.

* * *

To learn more about the Flagler Era (1894–1913) that followed the Pioneer Era, take the walking or biking tour in Chapter 2.

WALKING OR BIKING TOUR OF PALM BEACH AND WEST PALM BEACH DURING THE FLAGLER ERA (1894–1913)

This tour introduces the Flagler Era when Henry Morrison Flagler built his two grand hotels and residence in Palm Beach and laid out the downtown area of West Palm Beach. It can be done on foot or by bicycle.

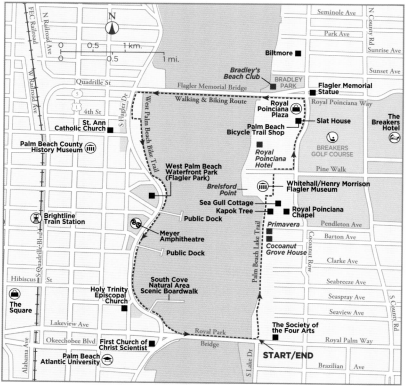

Map of Flagler Loop walking and biking tour

This tour is a 3-mile-long, counterclockwise loop on both sides of Lake Worth Lagoon between the Flagler Memorial Bridge and the Royal Park Bridge. The itinerary follows the 1-mile stretch of South Lake Trail in Palm Beach between the Royal Park Bridge (Middle Bridge) and the Flagler Memorial Bridge (North Bridge) where Henry Morrison Flagler built the grand Royal Poinciana Hotel and his residence Whitehall, then crosses to West Palm Beach on the Flagler Memorial Bridge that replaced the railroad bridge Flagler built in 1903 to transport his guests to his hotels in Palm Beach, then south 1 mile on the pedestrian and bike path alongside Flagler Drive past downtown West Palm Beach that was platted by Flagler in 1893, across the Royal Park Bridge back to Palm Beach and the beginning of South Lake Trail.

The tour starts at the southernmost end of South Lake Trail, alongside Lake Worth Lagoon at the bottom of the grass median in front of the Esther B. O'Keeffe Gallery Building of The Society of the Four Arts on Four Arts Plaza, just north of the Royal Park Bridge and Royal Palm Way. There are metered parking spaces for up to 2 hours on all streets between Seaview and Hammon Avenues, to be paid using the Park Mobile application (http://us.parkmobile.com). To park for more than 2 hours, paid parking is available at the Apollo Parking Lot at 405 Hibiscus Avenue just north of Worth Avenue, and at One Parking in The Esplanade at 150 Worth Avenue. Please do not park in the Four Arts parking lots and beware of spaces reserved for cars with parking permits. *Walking/biking instructions are in italics.* Commentary is not.

From the beginning of South Lake Trail, walk or bike a half-mile to the north. Just past the giant kapok tree, follow the trail to the right to Sea Gull Cottage, then immediately turn left and proceed to the entrance gate to the Henry Morrison Flagler Museum. Along the way, stop at the historical markers for the Cocoanut Row House (at the intersection with Pendleton Lane) and Sea Gull Cottage, and in front of the Flagler Museum, which are all described below.

Henry Morrison Flagler co-founded (with John D. Rockefeller) the Standard Oil Company in 1870. He spent the winter of 1878 in St. Augustine with his first wife. After retiring from Standard Oil in 1882, Flagler returned to St. Augustine with his second wife in 1883, when he decided to devote his energy and fortune to developing the east coast of Florida. He promptly set about constructing two hotels in St. Augustine and building a railroad down the east coast of Florida, appropriately named the Florida East Coast Railway. Prospecting for new destinations for his railroad and hotel businesses, Flagler first came to Palm Beach in 1892, only 20 years after the first pioneers

Henry Morrison Flagler
(1830–1913)

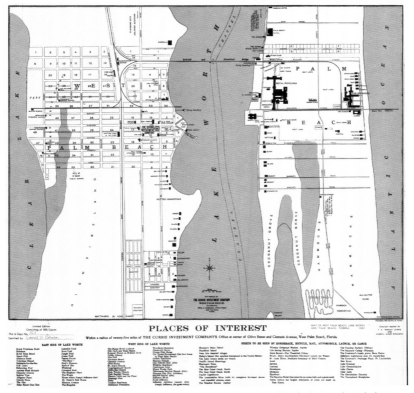

Excerpt of 1907 Currie Places of Interest Map, showing Flagler's two hotels in Palm Beach opposite the 48-block plat Flagler had laid out in a grid pattern for downtown West Palm Beach

settled along the east side of Lake Worth (see Chapter 1). He stayed in the Cocoanut Grove House, which pioneers Elisha and Ella Dimick had opened as the first hotel in the future Palm Beach in 1880.

Flagler resolved to make Palm Beach a resort for the well-to-do and bought land on both sides of the lake. He planned to build a resort hotel in Palm Beach for wealthy tourists from the north who would travel to Palm Beach on his railroad, and a new town on the west side of Lake Worth for commercial and residential purposes.

In 1892 Flagler bought **Croton Cottage** and the land around it from Denver businessman Robert McCormick. McCormick had purchased land from Elisha Newton's brother-in-law, Albert Geer, in 1886 and

Croton Cottage as seen from the top of the Royal Poinciana Hotel

built what was by far the best house on the lake at the time. Flagler lived there for 10 years before he moved next door into his grand new residence, Whitehall. (Croton Cottage was originally located around 100 yards north of where it stands today. It was later renamed **Sea Gull Cottage**.)

The same year Flagler also bought **Brelsford Point**, which juts out into Lake Worth, from the Brelsford brothers, who had opened the second general store in the Lake Worth Country, as the area was then known, in 1881. In 1887 the brothers opened the Palm Beach Post Office in their general store, giving Lake Worth Country its new name.

It was on Brelsford Point that Flagler commissioned the New York City architects John Carrère and Thomas Hastings to build the 55-room **Whitehall** in the Beaux-Arts style in 1902 as a wedding gift to his third wife, Mary Lily Kenan. Whitehall has housed the Henry Morrison Flagler Museum since 1960.

Whitehall under construction on Brelsford Point

Whitehall, as seen from the Royal Poinciana Hotel, circa 1910

The Royal Poinciana Hotel after the expansions of 1899 and 1901, with the first railway bridge between it and Whitehall on the right

On Cocoanut Row just south of the Flagler Museum and behind Sea Gull Cottage is the **Royal Poinciana Chapel**, originally called the Little Chapel, which Flagler built for hotel guests in 1897.

On May 1, 1893, 1,000 workers began construction of the Royal Poinciana Hotel, set back from the lake on the land Flagler had purchased from Robert McCormick. On February 11, 1894—less than

Guests enjoying afternoon tea in the Cocoanut Grove in front of the Royal Poinciana Hotel

10 months later—the 540-room **Royal Poinciana Hotel** opened. The hotel was an immediate success and was expanded in 1899 and again in 1901, making the Royal Poinciana the world's largest wooden hotel, its 1,081 rooms accommodating 2,000 guests. The hotel extended from Whitehall north to the Flagler Memorial Bridge, straddling what is now Cocoanut Row.

The Breakers

On the ocean side of Palm Beach directly opposite the Royal Poinciana Hotel, Flagler built a second hotel, originally called the Wayside Inn, then the Palm Beach Inn, and finally, **The Breakers** after a 1901 expansion because guests requested rooms "over by the breakers." The two hotels were connected by **Pine Walk** (the western part of which is now named Cocoanut Walk), which was—and still is—lined with Australian pine trees. The wood-frame Breakers burned down in 1903, but a new and larger hotel was built on the site in only eight months, again with a wood frame. That hotel burned down in 1925. It was replaced by the current twin-towered, 425-room hotel made of reinforced concrete, which opened in December 1926. For more information about The Breakers with vintage photographs, please refer to the Historic Driving Tour of Palm Beach in Chapter 4.

From the entrance to the Flagler Museum, continue walking or biking to the end of the high wrought-iron fence in front of Whitehall, cross Whitehall Way, and turn right onto the wide, paved path on the sidewalk on the far side of the street that is the continuation of South Lake Trail. At the corner, turn left on the path alongside Cocoanut Row and continue 200 yards to the historic marker for the Royal Poinciana Hotel that is beside the road just past the driveway to the Palm Beach Towers. Then continue 50 yards to the building with the octagonal atrium, known as the Slat House (where the Palm Beach Bicycle Shop is located), on the left.

The Slat House is the low building in the shape of a cross on the left between the six-story wings of the Royal Poinciana Hotel. It is now an office building. The Breakers was built directly opposite the original wings of the Royal Poinciana Hotel. The two hotels were connected by Pine Walk (lined with double rows of Australian pine trees) on their south side. The Whitehall Hotel, with its 11-story tower, is on the lower right side.

In 1897 Flagler built a 9-hole golf course between his two hotels. It was enlarged to 18 holes in 1901.

After a section connecting the main building of the Royal Poinciana Hotel to the north wing was damaged during the 1928 hurricane, it was demolished and replaced by a new greenhouse with an octagonal center that became known as the **"Slat House."**

Changes to Flagler Era Palm Beach 1934–1958

 For more information and vintage photographs about the changes to Flagler Era Palm Beach, please refer to the section entitled "Changes to Flagler Era Palm Beach 1934–1958" at the end of the Driving Tour of Historic Palm Beach in Chapter 4, much of which is repeated below.

The wood-framed Royal Poinciana Hotel, which occupied nearly the entire space between Whitehall and the Flagler Memorial Bridge, closed in 1930. Materials from the hotel were sold and used in more than 500 local buildings. The Royal Poinciana Hotel was finally demolished in 1934-35, 40 years after it was built; only the Slat House and the adjacent giant Mysore fig tree were spared. With its enormous, exposed roots and 150-foot branch spread, the Mysore fig tree (sometimes called a banyan or ficus tree) at the southern edge of the parking lot of Royal Poinciana Plaza is the largest of its kind in Palm Beach.

After the demolition of the Royal Poinciana Hotel, Cocoanut Row was extended to connect Royal Palm Way with the new Royal Poinciana Way.

The former site of the Royal Poinciana Hotel remained vacant for 20 years. In 1950 the Phipps family's Bessemer Properties acquired the Royal Poinciana property west of Cocoanut Row from the Florida East Coast Hotel Company for commercial development. Bessemer sold the southern portion of the property to developers who built the **Palm Beach Towers** at 44 Cocoanut Row in 1956. In 1958 Bessemer built the Regency-style **Royal Poinciana Plaza** shopping center and the 900-seat **Royal Poinciana Playhouse** on the 12 acres to the north; both were designed by John Volk. Royal Poinciana Plaza was renovated with new landscaping in 2016. The Royal Poinciana Playhouse was rebuilt starting in 2023 and is expected to reopen in 2025.

Continue walking or biking north past Royal Poinciana Plaza to the southwest corner of Royal Poinciana Way and Cocoanut Row.

When the Royal Poinciana Hotel first opened in 1894, the train depot was on the west shore of Lake Worth and guests took a ferry

The Florida East Coast Railway Bridge looking east to Palm Beach in 1937, the year before it was demolished and replaced by the Flagler Memorial Bridge

across to Palm Beach. Between 1894 and 1896, a 1,200-foot railroad bridge was built across Lake Worth, with a lane added for pedestrians and wheelchairs, so the train could deliver guests directly to the south side of the Royal Poinciana Hotel, where they were greeted by an orchestra. The wealthiest guests often arrived in their own railway cars, which were parked on the sidings of the hotel station during their stay. When the new Mrs. Flagler complained about the noise and smell of the trains next to Whitehall, her husband obligingly had the bridge moved to the north side of the hotel in 1903, where today's Flagler Memorial Bridge is located.

The train station in Palm Beach was located on what is now the median strip of Royal Poinciana Way. The train tracks were located on what are now the eastbound lanes of Royal Poinciana Way. The westbound lanes were originally named **Main Street**.

In 1938 the first **Flagler Memorial Bridge** replaced the second Florida East Coast Railway Bridge built by Flagler in 1903; a landscaped median replaced the train station; a second, east-west, street

Looking east on Main Street in the 1930s. Note the triangular tympanum of the Garden Theater (1921), now at 215 Royal Poinciana Way. It is one of the very few early buildings on Main Street still standing.

The Flagler Memorial Bridge is under construction, with the ferry terminal at its base, and the roof of the Beach Club in the lower right corner.

Colonel E. R. Bradley's Beach Club, circa 1930

replaced the railroad tracks; and Main Street and the new street were renamed **Royal Poinciana Way** (even though the way was lined with royal palm trees). Cocoanut Row was extended to connect Royal Palm Way and Royal Poinciana Way.

Look across Royal Poinciana Way at Bradley Park along Lake Worth Lagoon.

This is the site where, in 1898, Colonel Edward R. "E.R." Bradley opened **the Beach Club**, a dining club and gambling casino built to cater to guests of the Royal Poinciana Hotel and The Breakers. Bradley built his own house just north of the casino. Bradley's Beach Club closed after 48 years in 1945 and Bradley himself died the following year. His wife having predeceased him and being childless, Bradley willed the 4.5 acres of land where both his casino and adjacent house stood to the Town of Palm Beach for a public park. A wall and pagoda-style mantel and fireplace from his house were saved and are now located on the north side of the park, where they are known as the Bradley Pavilion. The park was enlarged and improved in 2017 following the construction of the new Flagler Memorial Bridge.

West Palm Beach during the Flagler Era

Walk or bike across Flagler Memorial Bridge on the sidewalk on the eastbound side to avoid having to cross busy Royal Poinciana Way. On the West Palm Beach side of the bridge, turn left onto the sidewalk on the east side of Flagler Drive and continue south along the sidewalk for 5 blocks to Banyan Street, where a wider pedestrian and bike path begins alongside Lake Worth Lagoon that continues to the Royal Park Bridge and well beyond. Both pedestrians and cyclists should follow the path for 2 blocks to the bottom of the park which is directly across the lake from the Flagler Museum.*

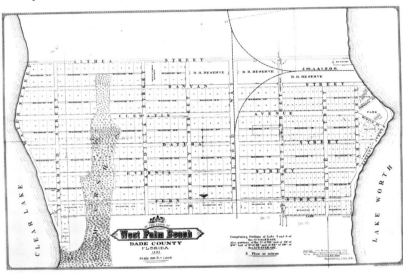

1893 Plat for the Town of West Palm Beach

While building the Royal Poinciana Hotel in Palm Beach on the east side of Lake Worth, Henry Flagler purchased land on the west side of the lake and hired the early pioneer George Potter, who among his many occupations was the Dade County surveyor, to lay out the new town, aptly called "West Palm Beach," for the people and businesses that would support Palm Beach. Flagler filed Potter's 48-block plat for the Town of West Palm Beach, extending east to west from Lake Worth to Clear Lake, with Dade County in November 1893. The streets were laid out in a grid pattern and named in alphabetical order after trees, fruits, and flowers that grew in the area. Running east-west were Althea, Banyan, Clematis, Datura, Evernia, and Fern Streets. The north-south streets were Lantana, Narcissus, Olive, Poinsettia, Rosemary, Sapodilla, and Tamarind. The only variation from the grid pattern was at the eastern end of Clematis, where the triangular City Park (later renamed **Flagler Park**) was laid out. The roads were first covered with crushed oyster shells; crushed coquina rock was later used for the principal thoroughfares. This platted area is still the center of West Palm Beach.

West Palm Beach, looking north past downtown to the Florida East Coast Railway Bridge, circa 1920

Continue south alongside Lake Worth Lagoon to the Royal Park Bridge. At the corner of the bridge, both pedestrians and cyclists should hug the sidewalk to the right to take the sidewalk on the north (westbound) side of the bridge before crossing the bridge to the foot of Royal Palm Way in Palm Beach. (The fork that goes to the left on the West Palm Beach side of the bridge goes under the bridge and continues south alongside South Flagler Drive.)

View, from left to right, of the Biltmore, the Royal Poinciana Hotel, and the White-hall Hotel from Flagler Drive in West Palm Beach in the late 1920s. Flagler Park is at the middle left.

The tour ends where it started on the Palm Beach side at the beginning of South Lake Trail.

Flagler's Architectural Legacy

Flagler died in Palm Beach in 1913. His third wife and widow, Mary Lily Kenan Flagler, remarried in 1916 and died in 1917. She left Whitehall to her niece, Louise Clisby Wise Lewis, who in 1924 sold Whitehall to new owners who converted it into a hotel. In 1926 they added a 10-story, 250-room tower behind the original building. In 1959, Flagler's granddaughter Jean Flagler Matthews bought the Whitehall

The Breakers at the bottom center with the Casino to the left and the cottages to the right; the Royal Poinciana Hotel at the top, with the Slat House in the gap on the right between the 6-story residential wings; Whitehall at the top left, with the 10-story tower that had been added in 1927 after it became a hotel; the FEC bridge from West Palm Beach on the top right, leading to Main Street. The Breakers and the Casino were both built in the 1920s, after Flagler's death. The Royal Poinciana Hotel was demolished in 1935. The FEC bridge was replaced by the Flagler Memorial Bridge in 1938. The cottages next to The Breakers were replaced by the Breakers Row condominiums in 1976 and 1986, and The Breakers Casino was replaced by The Breakers Beach Club in 1999. Today all that remains of Flagler's architectural legacy are Whitehall (now the Henry Morrison Flagler Museum) and the Slat House.

Whitehall in 1902

Hotel, tore down the tower, and restored the mansion to its former glory. The **Henry Morrison Flagler Museum** opened in 1960. It was a fitting tribute to the man whose impact on the Town of Palm Beach and the State of Florida is without equal.

In another tribute, an 11-foot-high bronze statue of Henry Morrison Flagler stands at the bottom of the median strip of Royal Poinciana Way, facing the new Flagler Memorial Bridge that opened in 2017.

* * *

The Walking Tour of Midtown Palm Beach in Chapter 3 introduces you to Palm Beach after the Flagler Era, taking you from where the Flagler Tour ends through the Royal Palm Addition, which was laid out between 1908 and 1918, and became the center of Palm Beach in the 1920s.

WALKING TOUR OF MIDTOWN PALM BEACH DURING THE BOOM TIMES OF THE 1920s

This walk covers the Royal Park Addition roughly between Royal Palm Way and Worth Avenue, which was laid out in the 1910s and was mainly developed during the real estate boom of the 1920s. The Royal Park Addition, now commonly known as Midtown, soon replaced Main Street of the Flagler Era as the center of Palm Beach.

Many of the sights mentioned in this walk are included in the Driving Tour of Historic Palm Beach in Chapter 4.

The walk starts and finishes at the southeast corner of Royal Palm Way and South Lake Drive, at the foot of the Royal Park Bridge. There are metered parking spaces for up to 2 hours on all streets between Seaview and Hammon Avenues, to be paid using the Park Mobile application (http://us.parkmobile.com). To park for more than 2 hours, paid parking is available at the Apollo Parking Lot at 405 Hibiscus Avenue just north of Worth Avenue, and at One Parking in The Esplanade at 150 Worth Avenue. Please do not park in the Four Arts parking lots and beware of spaces reserved for cars with parking permits.

Walking instructions are in italics. Commentary is not.

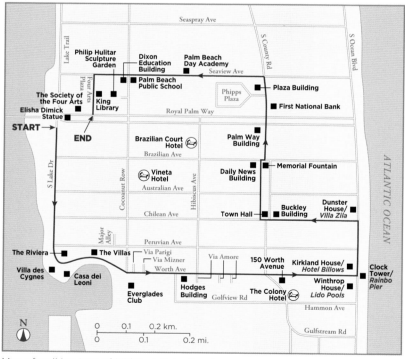

Map of walking tour of Midtown Palm Beach

Statue of Elisha Newton Dimick, the first mayor of Palm Beach, at the bottom of Royal Palm Way

Look at the statue of Elisha Dimick that stands in the median of Royal Palm Way, facing the Royal Park Bridge.

Elisha Newton "Cap" Dimick's impact on Palm Beach was second only to that of Henry Morrison Flagler. After moving with his young family from Michigan to Lake Worth Country in 1876, he played a leading role in the development of the Town of Palm Beach, opening its first hotel (Cocoanut Grove House, which was featured in Chapter 1), co-founding its first bank, and serving as its first mayor from 1911 to 1918, the year before his death at age 70. Elisha Dimick was also largely responsible for the development of the Royal Park Addition that moved Palm Beach from the Flagler Era (1894–1913) to a full-fledged town and not just a hotel destination.

During the Flagler Era, Palm Beach was firmly centered around the Royal Poinciana Hotel and The Breakers. The only bridge was the Florida East Coast railroad bridge, which led to Main Street (now Royal Poinciana Way). The area south of Flagler's grand hotels was full of lagoons and hammocks.

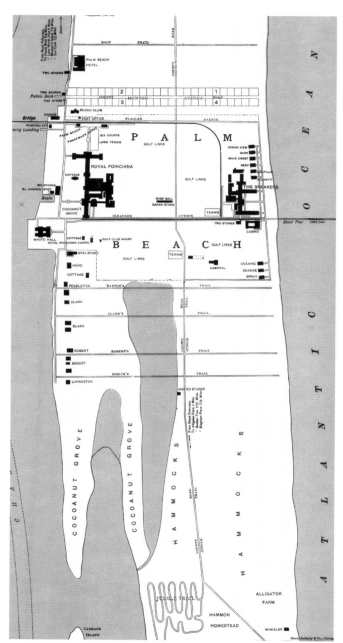

Excerpt of 1907 Currie Places of Interest Map showing County Road, Jungle Trail, and Alligator Joe's Alligator Farm during the Flagler Era. Note that the Alligator Farm was on the lake, not the ocean as shown on the map. The lagoons between Cocoanut Grove and Hammocks would be filled in.

Jungle Trail

There were few automobiles in Palm Beach during the Flagler Era. Guests at Flagler's two hotels would explore the island by walking, bicycling, or being pedaled in a wheelchair along the winding path cut through the dense tropical vegetation known as **"Jungle Trail,"** which went as far south as today's Worth Avenue and led to **Alligator Joe's alligator farm** on the lake. It was one of the most popular Palm Beach tourist attractions in the early 1900s. The owner, Warren Frazee, entertained the crowds by wrestling alligators. He died in 1915.

Alligator Joe at his alligator farm

Things changed with the opening of the Royal Park Addition and the Royal Park Bridge 1 mile south of the FEC railroad bridge (today the Flagler Memorial Bridge). Roads were built and the automobile finally appeared on the island. Seasonal residents started to move out of the grand hotels and build homes and clubs. Churches and commercial and public buildings soon followed.

Royal Park Addition

In 1908 pioneer Elisha Dimick and other investors purchased 160 acres to develop the **Royal Park Addition**, one of the first two subdivisions in Palm Beach (the other was the Floral Park Addition just north of Royal Poinciana Way). The property extended from Lake Worth to the ocean and roughly from Seaview Avenue to Golfview Road. They built a bulkhead for Lake Worth, hauled tons of beach sand to fill in marshy areas, and built 4.5 miles of roads, including the five parallel avenues south of Royal Palm Way: Brazilian, Australian, Chilean, Peruvian, and Worth. (Brazilian is wider than the other avenues since it was originally intended to be a commercial street.) Most importantly, in 1911—the same year that the Town of Palm Beach was incorporated—they built the **Royal Park Bridge**, originally a wooden toll bridge that accommodated automobiles, which led directly from West Palm Beach to the foot of Royal Palm Way. By 1918 the Royal Park Addition was completely laid out and mostly sold, World War I ended, and construction began in earnest.

Look east up Royal Palm Way.

REVISED MAP OF ROYAL PARK ADDITION TO PALM BEACH, FLORIDA

Map of Royal Park Addition

The bottom of Royal Palm Way faces Royal Park Bridge.

Royal Palm Way with mature royal palm trees

Elisha Dimick's house on Royal Palm Way

Royal Palm Way was the grand entrance to the Royal Park Addition, running the entire width of the development, intersecting with South County Road, and ending at South Ocean Boulevard, the town's principal north-south thoroughfares. Its broad median was flanked by two rows of royal palm trees. After the new Royal Park Addition opened in 1911, the investors built their own homes on the street, which were the first houses in the neighborhood.

Royal Palm Way was lined with houses until the zoning changed from predominantly residential to commercial in 1973, when office buildings started to be constructed, resulting in the "Bankers Row" that it is today.

With the construction of Ocean Boulevard (1912–1916), the Royal Park Bridge, and Royal Palm Way, the automobile finally arrived in Palm Beach.

Walk south on South Lake Drive past the Town of Palm Beach Marina, sometimes called the Town Docks.

Follow South Lake Drive as it turns left (east) and becomes Worth Avenue. Continue walking on Worth Avenue.

When you turn left onto Worth Avenue, on the right, overlooking the Lake Worth Lagoon are two of Addison Mizner's earliest commissions: **Casa dei Leoni (House of Lions)** at 450 Worth Avenue (built

Lakeside Condos and Nearby Hotels

In its correct chronological order, the following discussion should appear after the discussion below about the Everglades Club on Worth Avenue, but it appears here because it deals with the geographical area between Royal Palm Way and Worth Avenue, and west of South County Road, that you are walking by on your way to the Everglades Club.

The **Town Docks** were built in the 1940s, were upgraded in 1998, and underwent a major expansion in 2021. The adjacent **Lake Drive Park** was renovated at the same time.

On the east side of South Lake Drive, architect Howard Chilton designed 6-story-high apartment buildings at 369 (1957), 389 (1958), and 315 (1961) South Lake Drive. (He built a total of 15 apartment buildings between Royal Palm Way and Worth Avenue.) These and other apartment buildings replaced single-family bungalows that were first built in this section of the Royal Park Addition, a handful of which still exist today.

Two new hotels were also built in the residential area of the Royal Park Addition between South County Road and South Lake Drive:

The Brazilian Court Hotel with its original entrance on Brazilian Avenue on the right side

The **Brazilian Court Hotel**, now at 301 Australian Avenue, opened on January 1, 1926. The site originally consisted of a few bungalows. Italian-born architect Rosario Candela designed a 2-story complex of 116 apartments built around a courtyard. Maurice Fatio made substantial additions in 1936. The original entrance was on Brazilian Avenue but was later moved to Australian Avenue.

The **Lido-Venice Hotel** opened at 363 Cocoanut Row in 1926. From 1928 until 1977 the hotel was known as **The Vineta** before it was renamed, under new ownership, the Royal Park. In 1980, the hotel was converted into condos, and by 1985 was operating as a hotel condominium known as the Palm Court. In 1989, it became the **Chesterfield Hotel** with new owners, renowned for its Leopard Lounge. It changed hands again in 2022, and after renovation, the hotel will once again reopen as the Vineta Hotel.

The Colony Hotel on Hammon Avenue in 1962. Behind it along the ocean are, from left to right, the Sea Glade Hotel (originally named Hotel Billows), the Rainbo Pier, and Lido Pools, all at the eastern end of Worth Avenue, all of which were demolished by 1970.

To round out the list of historic hotels in the midtown area, the 6-story Colony Hotel, designed by Byron Simonson and originally called the Golfview, opened at the corner of Hammon Avenue and South County Road in 1947.

Villa des Cygnes

The Riviera, designed by architect John Stetson in 1955 Jed Lyons

for Leonard Thomas in 1921), and **Villa des Cygnes (House of the Swans)** at 456 Worth Avenue (built for Barclay Warburton in 1922).

On your left, at 455 Worth Avenue, is **The Riviera,** an apartment building that was designed by architect John Stetson in 1951.

Farther along on your left, overlooking the lagoon, the 6-story **Villas** cooperative apartment building was constructed at 425 Worth Avenue in 1971.

Behind the Villas, at 417 Peruvian Avenue, is **Major Alley**, a collection of six small Bermuda-style row houses built by Howard Major in 1925 as a reaction against Mizner's Mediterranean Revival style.

One block farther to the east, at 311 Peruvian Avenue, is the **Preservation Foundation of Palm Beach**, which was founded in 1980 to preserve the town's architectural heritage. The building was constructed in 2005. The adjacent Pan's Garden, Florida's first all-native botanical garden, was established in 1994.

Walk to the far corner of Worth Avenue and Cocoanut Row.

Boom Time

After World War I, Palm Beach—and all south Florida—experienced a building boom, with the construction of homes, clubs, churches, and commercial and public buildings at a frenetic pace. Virtually all the buildings that give Palm Beach its distinctive style were built during the period between the two wars, but especially during the Roaring Twenties. The great architects of the day—Addison Mizner, Maurice Fatio, Joseph Urban, Marion Sims Wyeth, Howard Major, Gustav Maass, and John Volk—all got their starts during this period.

It all began with the Everglades Club at the western end of Worth Avenue.

The Everglades Club when it first opened in 1919

Aerial view of the Everglades Club when it first opened in 1919

The Everglades Club and Worth Avenue

From the northeast corner of Cocoanut Row and Worth Avenue, look across the street at the north façade of the Everglades Club.

The original north façade of the Everglades Club on Worth Avenue, looking east

Looking east up Worth Avenue with the new north façade of the Everglades Club under construction on the right, and the arcades under construction on the left (December 15, 1925)

The new north façade of the Everglades Club on Worth Avenue, looking east

In 1917 Paris Singer, the 23rd child of Isaac Merritt Singer, inventor of the Singer sewing machine, purchased the land on the shores of Lake Worth where Alligator Joe had his alligator farm, which was a popular tourist attraction during the Flagler Era. He brought architect Addison Mizner to Palm Beach in January 1918 to design what became the private **Everglades Club**, which opened in January 1919. Singer expanded the club's facilities and added apartments, including a tower for his residence. Mizner built a new façade along Worth Avenue in 1925. Mizner's distinctive design—called Mediterranean Revival—created the look that was to become most closely associated with Palm Beach.

In 1923 **Worth Avenue**, then a dirt road, was named after General William Jenkins Worth, the last commander of US forces during the Second Seminole War (1835–1842). (The lake had been named after him in 1841.)

Cross Worth Avenue and look back at the arcades on the north side of the street.

In 1924-25 Singer commissioned Mizner to design the first shopping arcades at the western end of Worth Avenue, including **Via**

The shopping arcades under construction in 1925 across from the Everglades Club, looking north, with the future Via Parigi, Via Mizner, and Villa Mizner at the right

Aerial view of the Everglades Club and Worth Avenue in 1937

Aerial view of the Everglades Club and its golf course, with Worth Avenue leading to the Rainbo Pier, in 1939

Parigi (Paris in Italian) and **Via Mizner**. Mizner lived in the tower and adjoining apartment on Via Mizner, called **Villa Mizner**, and had his studio on the second floor of the building to the east.

Cross Worth Avenue. Meander through Via Mizner and Via Parigi, admiring the connecting inner courtyards, and return to Worth Avenue. Start walking east on Worth Avenue, toward the ocean.

In the 1920s and 1930s, the commercial development of Worth Avenue moved east from the Everglades Club and Mizner's arcades.

During the early 1930s, Worth Avenue featured as many as eight automobile showrooms. The Cadillac showroom that opened in 1928 is now occupied by the clothing store Maus & Hoffman at 312 Worth Avenue.

Worth Avenue looking east from the corner of Hibiscus Avenue, circa 1930s. The Hodges Building at 300 Worth Avenue is the 4-story building on the left.

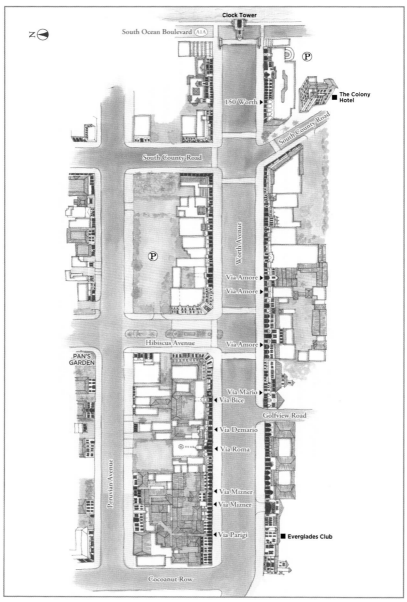

Map of Worth Avenue

In 1927 Velma Glenn Hodges built the **Hodges Building** at 300 Worth Avenue. Its first tenant, Saks Fifth Avenue, remained for over 50 years.

In addition to Mizner's original Via Parigi and Via Mizner, there are six other "vias" off of Worth Avenue to explore at your leisure, including, heading east, Via Roma, Via Demario, Via Bice, and Via Encantada, all on the north side of Worth Avenue, and Via Mario and Via Amore, both on the south side of Worth Avenue. Via Amore is the largest of the vias. It is built around connecting courtyards lined with shops and has three entrances. The center and principal entrance is directly opposite Hibiscus Avenue at 256 Worth Avenue.

Enter Via Amore at 256 Worth Avenue, walk east through the court-yards past Café Flora, and exit Via Amore at the easternmost entrance at 240 Worth Avenue. Continue walking east on Worth Avenue.

Kassatly's clothing and linen boutique, at 250 Worth Avenue, opened in 1923 and is the oldest shop on Worth Avenue.

The Greenleaf & Crosby jewelry store at 236 Worth Avenue, with its distinctive black and silver art deco façade, was built in 1932. (Greenleaf & Crosby was acquired by Betteridge in 2006.)

The bar at Ta-boo in 1945

Volunteers for Victory's Soldier Canteen at 416 South County Road in 1944

In 1941 Ted Stone opened the "Ta-boo" restaurant on Worth Avenue. With a retractable roof for dancing under the stars and a circular bamboo bar, Ta-boo was the place to go in the 1940s and 1950s. The restaurant changed owners several times and moved to 221 Worth Avenue in 1990. Ta-boo closed in 2023, but a new Ta-boo restaurant under new ownership is expected to open on the same site in 2025.

Between 1942 and 1945 a canteen for the enlisted men who were stationed in and around Palm Beach for training before being shipped overseas was run by the local **Volunteers for Victory** organization in an old Butterfield's grocery store building on the northwest corner of Worth Avenue and South County Road.

Worth Avenue in the late 1950s, looking west from South County Road, with the new Worth Avenue Building on the right

In 1955 architect John Stetson built the Armour Building (later renamed the **Worth Avenue Building**) on the site of the Volunteers for Victory's Soldier Canteen.

Cross South County Road and continue walking east on Worth Avenue to the clock tower on South Ocean Boulevard.

The block between County Road and South Ocean Boulevard only became a retail shopping area with the construction of the Esplanade (now called **150 Worth Avenue**) in 1980. Before then it was lined with houses.

Aerial view of the Everglades Club and Worth Avenue with the Rainbo Pier at the top in the 1950s

At the eastern end of Worth Avenue, cross South Ocean Boulevard and walk to the clock tower.

Ocean Boulevard, originally called Gulf Stream Drive, opened in 1916 after four years of construction. It ran along the ocean bluff for nearly its entire 23-mile length from Lake Worth Inlet to Delray.

Drawing of the Esplanade on Worth Avenue, 1979

Lido, Rainbo, Condo

The **clock tower** at the eastern end of Worth Avenue, which was built during a makeover of Worth Avenue in 2010, marks the former location of the 1,000-foot-long **Rainbo Pier,** which was built by Gus Jordahn in 1924. The pier was damaged by storms and was finally demolished in 1969.

On the southwest corner of Worth Avenue and South Ocean Boulevard, Jordahn built the **"Welcome to Our Ocean"** pool in 1914. It was one of the first commercial buildings constructed in the new Royal Park Addition. In the 1920s Jordahn enlarged the facility and changed the name to **"Gus' Baths."** New owners renamed it **"Lido Pools"** in 1931. The bathhouse and pools were demolished in 1970, and the Winthrop House condominium was built on the site by developer Michael Burrows.

On the northwest corner of Worth Avenue and South Ocean Boulevard, across the street from Gus' Baths, the **Hotel Billows** opened in December 1923. It was designed by William Manly King and was the first hotel in Palm Beach to remain open year-round. After the Hotel Billows went bankrupt in 1933, the new owners renovated the property and reopened it as the Sea Glade Hotel. It was demolished and

Gus' Baths opened in 1914, just south of what would become Worth Avenue.

Aerial view of Lido Pools on South Ocean Boulevard between Hammon Avenue on the left and Worth Avenue on the right, with its two saltwater swimming pools. The pools were drained and refilled with fresh seawater every 48 hours. The pool on the right is empty.

Aerial view of South Ocean Boulevard with Lido Pools at the bottom right and the Hotel Billows above it, on the far side of Worth Avenue. The entrance to the Rainbo Pier is at the center right.

The Villa Zila stood on South Ocean Boulevard between Chilean and Australian Avenues.

the Kirkland House condominium was built on the site by Michael Burrows in 1974.

Walk 2 blocks north along South Ocean Boulevard to Chilean Avenue.

The half-mile between Worth Avenue and Royal Palm Way beyond the Winthrop House and the Kirkland House is lined with more condominiums built during the 1960s and 1970s, including the following buildings (from south to north):

- The 400 Building, 400 South Ocean Boulevard, designed by Edward Durrell Stone in 1963.
- Dunster House, 360 South Ocean Boulevard, built by Michael Burrows in 1978 on the site of the **Villa Zila**, a house built in 1914 in the Prairie Modern style associated with Frank Lloyd Wright that was later converted into the Shorewinds Motor Hotel.
- Lowell House, 340 South Ocean Boulevard, built by Michael Burrows in 1975.
- 300 South Ocean Boulevard, designed by Howard Chilton in 1960.
- 100 Royal Palm Way, designed by Howard Chilton in 1969, and built on the former site of La Fontana, a mansion designed by Addison Mizner for George Luke Mesker in 1923.

Turn left on Chilean Avenue and walk one block west to South County Road.

Town Hall Square Historic District

In the decade following the opening of the Everglades Club in 1919, the center of gravity of Palm Beach permanently shifted south to the Royal Park Addition from Main Street and Flagler's grand hotels. To make the shift south official, the **Town Hall** and the adjacent fire station (both designed by the West Palm Beach architectural firm of Harvey and Clarke) were built in the center of the Royal Park Addition in 1925 (the two buildings were connected in 1967 and the fire station moved to a new building across the street), and the **Memorial Fountain** (designed by Addison Mizner and dedicated to honor Henry Morrison Flagler and Elisha Newton Dimick) was built in front of the original fire station in 1930 (it was restored in 2016).

Town Hall

The Daily News Building at the southwest corner of South County Road and Brazilian Avenue

Harvey and Clarke also designed many of the commercial buildings located on South County Road in or near Town Hall Square, including the **Buckley Building** (365 South County Road), the **Daily News Building** (204 Brazilian Avenue), and the **Palm Way Building** (288 South County Road).

Note the Buckley Building at the northeast corner of Chilean Avenue and South County Road, opposite the south end of the Town Hall.

Cross to the west side of South County Road and walk north toward Royal Palm Way.

Note, in order along the way, the Town Hall and Memorial Fountain in the median, The Daily News Building at the southwest corner of Brazilian Avenue, and the Palm Way Building at the southwest corner of Royal Palm Way.

At the southwest corner of South County Road and Royal Palm Way, look at the yellow building around 100 yards to the right on the far side of the ocean block at 151 Royal Palm Way with the name of the Gunster law firm on the front.

Memorial Fountain, in memory of Henry Morrison Flagler and Elisha Newton Dimick, was designed by Addison Mizner.

This is the last of the single-family houses first built on Royal Palm Way. It is now used as an office building.

Cross Royal Palm Way, walk halfway down the block and look at the bank across the street.

Landmarks from the 1920s

Near the northeast corner of South County Road and Royal Palm Way stands the **First National Bank Building** (255 South County Road), now occupied by Wells Fargo. Maurice Fatio designed the first building on the site in 1925. Marion Sims Wyeth designed the original First National Bank Building at 255 South County Road in 1927. John Volk designed the neoclassical addition on the north side of the building in 1937 and replaced Wyeth's Moorish façade with another neoclassical temple front in 1955. (John Volk was the most prolific architect in Palm Beach, completing over 1,000 commissions between his arrival in Palm

The First National Bank Building in 1940

The Plaza Building on the west side of South County Road, next to the entrance to Phipps Plaza

Beach in 1925 and his death in 1984.) The entire group of six buildings between Royal Palm Way and Seaview Avenue was renovated in 2017.

Continue walking north on South County Road to the entrance to Phipps Plaza on your left.

In 1924 the Phipps family's Palm Beach Company commissioned Addison Mizner to design the **Plaza Building** on the north side of the entrance to Phipps Plaza on South County Road. The Plaza Building, where shops like Bonwit Teller and Brooks Brothers were located, became the anchor for **Phipps Plaza**, a combination of residential and commercial buildings constructed around an elliptically shaped green space.

In 1930 Mizner designed the 2-story quarried-keystone office building on the south side of the entrance to Phipps Plaza, at **264 South County Road**, for the brokerage firm E.F. Hutton. It was one of his last commissions. Since 2022 it and the adjacent building at 270 South County Road, which was designed by Maurice Fatio, house the Carriage House Club.

Continue walking north on South County Road and turn left (west) at the first street, Seaview Avenue. Walk one long block past the Palm Beach Day Academy on your right and then Palm Beach Public School on your left, to Cocoanut Row.

Education and Culture

Palm Beach Day Academy

In 1921 the Palm Beach School for Boys and the Palm Beach School for Girls were established. In 1930 the two schools were combined into one and renamed Palm Beach Private School. The following year an art deco–style building was constructed for the school at 241 Seaview Avenue. In 1966 the school changed its name to the Palm Beach Day School. In 2006 the Palm Beach Day School merged with the Academy of the Palm Beaches, which had opened in 1981 in West Palm Beach. The new two-campus school was officially renamed the Palm Beach Day Academy.

Palm Beach Public School

In 1921 Palm Beach Public School, designed by T. H. Tremble, opened as a 2-room school on the southeast corner of Cocoanut Row and Seaview Avenue. It was enlarged in 1927 and served grades one through eight.

Cross Cocoanut Row.

The original building for The Society of the Four Arts is now the King Library.

Palm Beach Junior High School

In 1929 Palm Beach Junior High School was built on the west side of the street at 240 Cocoanut Row, serving grades seven through nine; it was designed by William Manly King. (The original building on the east side of Cocoanut Row became the elementary school.)

The Society of the Four Arts

In 2010 The Society of the Four Arts acquired the Palm Beach Junior High School building. After extensive renovations, it reopened in 2013 as the Fitz Eugene Dixon Education Building, which serves as the home of the Society's Campus on the Lake.

Continue walking west on Seaview Avenue. Turn left on Four Arts Plaza and stop in front of the King Library.

In 1936 The Society of the Four Arts was established. In 1938 the original Four Arts building (now the King Library) opened; it was designed by Maurice Fatio. The bronze sculptures of male and female panthers flanking its entrance were created in 1933 by American artist Wheeler Williams. The Four Arts Botanical Gardens were laid out on the south side of the building in the same year.

Look across the street at the long, low building that stretches from Four Arts Plaza nearly down to the lake, with an esplanade in front of it.

Addison Mizner designed the **Embassy Club**, a private nightclub at the west end of Royal Palm Way on the lake, for Edward R. Bradley. The club opened in 1930 but soon went bankrupt. The Society of the Four Arts purchased the Embassy Club from Bradley's estate

The Embassy Club at the bottom of Royal Palm Way, now the Esther B. O'Keefe Gallery Building of The Society of the Four Arts

in 1947 and engaged John Volk to redesign the building for performances and exhibitions. The open-air dance floor was converted into a 700-seat auditorium. During the renovation, the entrance was moved from Royal Palm Way to the north side of the building. It is now the Esther B. O'Keeffe Gallery Building. The original Four Arts building, designed by Maurice Fatio in 1938, became **The Society of the Four Arts King Library**.

Continue to the corner of Four Arts Plaza and Royal Palm Way.

In 1992 the Four Arts acquired the **Embassy Apartments** building (another 1924 Mizner design) at the corner of Four Arts Plaza and Royal Palm Way, where it installed the children's library and administration offices. It was renamed the John E. Rovensky Building.

Why not end your walking tour with a visit to the 2.17-acre **Philip Hulitar Sculpture Garden**, which opened in 1980 and includes sculptures by 20 world-renowned artists? The garden can be entered either through the King Library, via the entrance to the Four Arts Botanical Gardens which is immediately to the right (south) of the King Library, or via the gate opposite the entrance to the Dixon Education Building. The Sculpture Garden is open seven days a week from 10 a.m. to 5 p.m. Public toilets are available in the Pannill Pavilion. Admission is free of charge.

End of walking tour.

Royal Palm Way in the 1940s

CHAPTER 4

DRIVING TOUR OF HISTORIC PALM BEACH

This driving tour covers the history of Palm Beach from the Flagler Era (1894–1913) until today. The complete route goes as far north as the Lake Worth Inlet and as far south as Phipps Ocean Park—a distance of 10 miles.

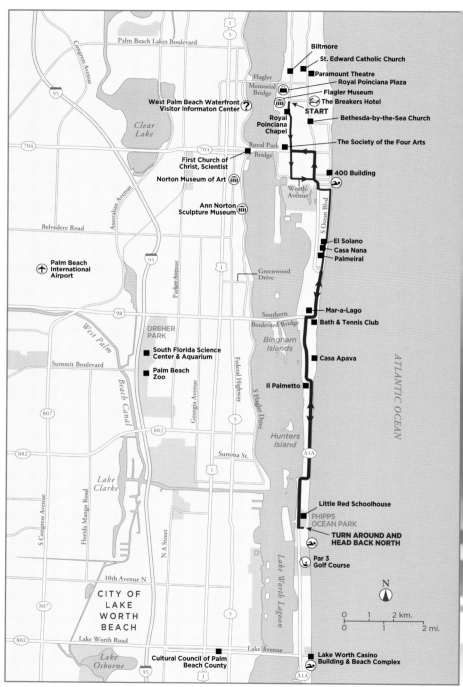

Maps of overview of southern and northern parts of the Driving Tour of Historic Palm Beach

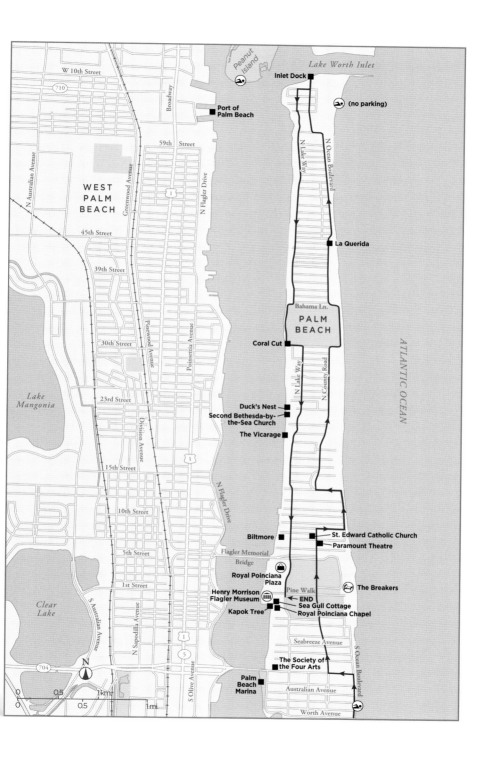

The driving tour starts and finishes at the Henry Morrison Flagler Museum at 1 Whitehall Way, off Cocoanut Row, and takes around two hours. It can be shortened by not going farther south than the roundabout at the east end of the Southern Boulevard Bridge, near the entrance to the Bath & Tennis Club at 1170 South Ocean Boulevard, or farther north than the Beach Club at 755 North County Road—a distance of 5 miles. *Driving instructions are in italics.* Commentary is not.

To discover the Pioneer Era (1870s–1894) that preceded the Flagler Era, before taking the driving tour you may wish to take at least the first part of the walking or biking tour on North Lake Trail in Chapter 1, from Bradley Park to the second Bethesda-by-the-Sea Episcopal Church, a one-way distance of 1.2 miles. The section of South Lake Trail that is particularly relevant to the Flagler Era—which includes the Cocoanut Grove House and the Sea Gull Cottage (both just south of the Flagler Museum), and Brelsford Point (on which the Flagler Museum is located), is summarized below.

The second Southern Boulevard Bridge opened in 1950. Its replacement opened in 2022. (The Bath & Tennis Club is below in the center. Mar-a-Lago is on the right.)

The Beginning of the Flagler Era

In 1876 Elisha Newton "Cap" Dimick and his wife Ella, his brother Frank and his wife Anna, their sister Marion and her husband Albert Geer (the three Dimick siblings had married three Geer siblings), and their parents moved to Lake Worth Country from Constantine, Michigan. Cap and Ella built their home on the lake. In 1880, they added eight rooms to their house to accommodate visitors and opened the first hotel on Lake Worth, and the first hotel between Titusville and Key West. The hotel was gradually enlarged to 50 rooms. They named the hotel the **Cocoanut Grove House** (using the old-fashioned spelling of "coconut") since it was located next to the grove of coconut palm trees that had been planted by the settlers in 1878 when the Spanish frigate *Providencia* ran aground south of today's Bath & Tennis Club with its cargo of 20,000 coconuts.

In 1880 Edward and John Brelsford purchased Bonefish Point from Frank Dimick, and thereafter it was known as **Brelsford Point,** and opened a General Store. The point protrudes into the lake around 200 yards north of where the Cocoanut Grove House stood. In 1887 they opened the "Palm Beach Post Office," in reference to the coconut

Cocoanut Grove House Avenue

palm trees that had been planted nine years earlier. In a few years, Palm Beach replaced Lake Worth Country as the name of the community on the east side of the lake.

In 1892 Henry Morrison Flagler made his first visit to Lake Worth and stayed at the Cocoanut Grove House. He resolved to extend his railroad, which began in Jacksonville, to Lake Worth and to make Palm Beach a resort for the well-to-do.

That same year Flagler bought **Croton Cottage** and the land around it from Denver businessman Robert McCormick. McCormick had purchased Albert Geer's land in 1886 and built what was by far the best house on the lake at the time.

In 1893 Flagler bought Brelsford Point from the Brelsford brothers, as well as land on the west side of the lake. He planned to build a resort hotel in Palm Beach and a new town on the west side of Lake Worth for commercial and residential purposes.

Flagler lived in Croton Cottage until he finished building the 55-room **Whitehall** on Brelsford Point in 1902 as a wedding gift to his third wife, Mary Lily Kenan. Croton Cottage was originally located around 100 yards north of where it stands today. It was later renamed Sea Gull Cottage.

The driving tour repeats much of the information about the Flagler Era that is included in Chapter 2.

The Flagler Era

From the Flagler Museum, drive east to Cocoanut Row. Turn left on Cocoanut Row and drive north past the Palm Beach Towers and the Royal Poinciana Plaza to Royal Poinciana Way.

On May 1, 1893, construction began on the **Royal Poinciana Hotel**. The six-story, 540-room hotel opened 10 months later. Additions were built in 1899 and 1901, making the Royal Poinciana the world's largest wooden hotel, its 1,081 rooms on 3 miles of corridors accommodating 2,000 guests. Nearly the entire distance between Whitehall Way and Royal Poinciana Way was originally occupied by Flagler's Royal Poinciana Hotel.

On the far side of what is now Royal Poinciana Way, in what is now Bradley Park along the lake, once stood the **Beach Club**, a dining club and gambling casino built by Colonel Edward R. "E.R." Bradley in

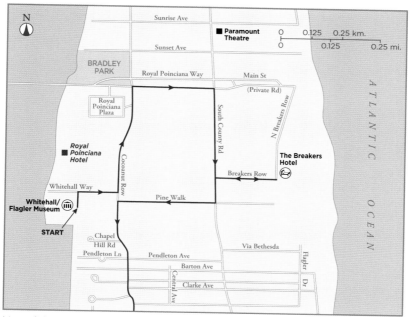

Map of the Flagler section of the driving tour

The first section of the Royal Poinciana Hotel on Lake Worth

The Royal Poinciana Hotel after the 1899 and 1901 extensions on the north side of the original hotel

1898 to cater to guests of the Royal Poinciana Hotel and The Breakers. Bradley built his own house just north of the casino.

Turn right on Royal Poinciana Way and drive to the stoplight at the end, at the junction with County Road.

When the Royal Poinciana Hotel first opened in 1894, the train depot was on the west shore of Lake Worth and guests took a ferry across to Palm Beach. Between 1894 and 1896, a 1,200-foot railroad

The Palm Beach Florida East Coast Railroad station in 1926

bridge was built across Lake Worth so the train could deliver guests directly to the south side of the Royal Poinciana Hotel, where they were greeted by an orchestra. When Whitehall was built on the other side of the railroad in 1902, Mrs. Flagler complained about the noise and smell, so her husband obligingly moved the railroad bridge to the north side of the hotel, where today's Flagler Memorial Bridge now stands. Passengers disembarked at a station located on what is now the median strip of Royal Poinciana Way. On the south side of today's Royal Poinciana Way were the railroad tracks. On the north side was Main Street.

Hotel guests beside the FEC train next to the Royal Poinciana Hotel

The original Wayside Inn on the ocean. The hotel was renamed The Breakers in 1901.

At the east end of Royal Poinciana Way, turn right on County Road and drive south to The Breakers. At the first stoplight turn left into the driveway, stop at the gatehouse, and tell the guard that you would like to drive to the fountain in front of the hotel and back to admire the hotel.

In 1896 Flagler built a second hotel, first named the Wayside Inn, this time on the oceanfront. The tracks of the railroad bridge that delivered guests to the south side of the Royal Poinciana Hotel in 1896 were extended to the south side of the Palm Beach Inn and then to the end of a 1,000-foot-long pier, where cargo and passengers could continue to Cuba or Nassau on Flagler's P&O Steamship Line. After a 1901 expansion, the hotel was renamed **The Breakers**. After the railroad bridge was moved to the north side of the Royal Poinciana Hotel in 1902, Flagler extended the railroad spur south from Main Street so that it passed in front of The Breakers, where guests could disembark. Thereafter "the great pier" was no longer used by trains. (It was damaged in the 1928 hurricane and its remains were demolished.)

The Breakers burned down in 1903. It was rebuilt, once again in wood, eight months later. The Breakers burned down a second time in 1925. It was replaced in just 11 months by the current twin-towered hotel, this time made of reinforced concrete, designed by the

The Breakers fire of June 9, 1903

The east side of the new Breakers Hotel overlooking the ocean in 1927

New York City architecture firm Schultze & Weaver and inspired by the Villa Medici in Rome.

Return to the entrance of The Breakers. Turn left (south) on County Road. In 200 yards, at the next stoplight, turn right on Cocoanut Walk and continue slowly west between two rows of Australian pine trees to Cocoanut Row.

Mule train between Palm Walk and Pine Walk

For a nickel, guests of the Royal Poinciana or The Breakers could shuttle between the two hotels on a mule-drawn trolley that ran on tracks parallel and between **Palm Walk** and **Pine Walk**. The trolley was retired in 1928 when the tracks were removed.

In 1897 Flagler built a 9-hole golf course between his two hotels. It was enlarged to 18 holes in 1901. Pine Walk still runs from The Breakers to Cocoanut Row.

The Little Church, now known as the Royal Poinciana Chapel

Turn left (south) on Cocoanut Row.

Shortly after turning, on your right you will pass the non-denominational **Royal Poinciana Chapel**, which Flagler built in 1897 for the guests at his two hotels. It was originally called the **Little Church**.

Continue south on Cocoanut Row to Royal Palm Way.

Clarke Trail in 1894

In 1894 there was a lily pond where Clarke Avenue crosses Cocoanut Row.

In 1893 Commodore Charles J. Clarke of Pittsburgh sailed his yacht *Alma* to Palm Beach and purchased the Cocoanut Grove House and 60 acres of vacant ocean-to-lake property from Elisha Dimick. Clarke's Trail crossed the property, roughly where Clarke Avenue stands today.

After the Cocoanut Grove House burned down in October 1893, Commodore Clarke built a house he named Primavera the following year.

At the corner of Seaview Avenue, you will pass the original two-room **Palm Beach Public School** (built in 1921) on the left, and what

Primavera

was originally the **Palm Beach Junior High School** (built in 1929) on the right. (The latter was acquired by The Society of the Four Arts and reopened after extensive renovations in 2013 as the Fitz Eugene Dixon Education Building, which serves as the home of the Society's Campus on the Lake.)

Royal Park Addition and the Beginning of the Property Boom

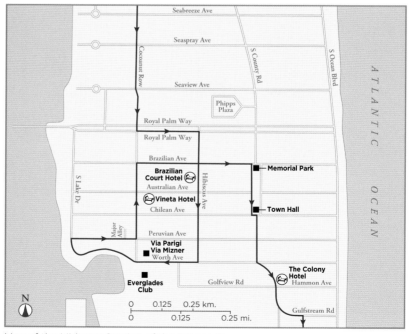

N.B. For a more complete description of the Royal Park Addition, refer to the walking tour with vintage photographs in Chapter 3.

In 1908 Elisha Dimick, the early pioneer who moved to Lake Worth Country in 1876 and opened the Cocoanut Grove House hotel on Lake Trail in 1880 (see Chapter 1), and other investors purchased 160 acres to develop the **Royal Park Addition**, one of the first two subdivisions in Palm Beach. The property extended from Lake Worth to the ocean and from Seaview Avenue to Golfview Road. They built a bulkhead for Lake Worth, hauled tons of beach sand to fill in marshy areas, and built 4.5 miles of roads, including the five parallel avenues south of Royal Palm Way: Brazilian, Australian,

Map of the Midtown Section of the Driving Tour

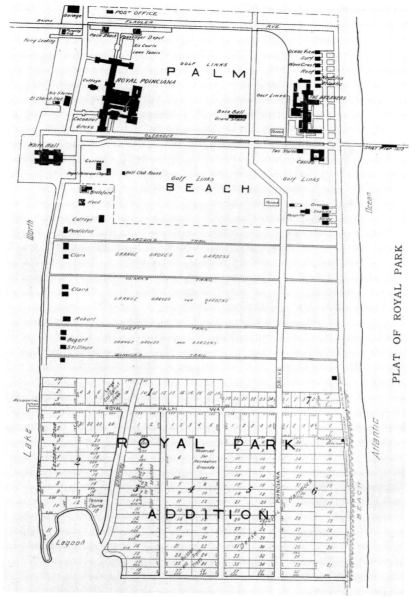

Plat of Royal Park Addition, circa 1913

Royal Palm Way, looking west toward the Royal Park Bridge, with mature royal palms, circa 1950

Chilean, Peruvian, and Worth. (Brazilian is wider than the other avenues since it was originally intended to be a commercial street.) Most importantly, in 1911 they built the **Royal Park Bridge**, originally a wooden toll bridge, which led directly from West Palm Beach to the foot of Royal Palm Way. By 1918 the Royal Park Addition was completely laid out and mostly sold, but only after World War I was over could construction begin in earnest.

Royal Palm Way was the grand entrance to the Royal Park Addition, running the entire width of the development, intersecting with South County Road and ending at South Ocean Boulevard, the town's principal north-south thoroughfares. Its broad median was lined with

Seabreeze Avenue in 1926

royal palm trees. The investors built their own homes on the street, which were the first houses in the neighborhood. A statue of Elisha Dimick, who was also Palm Beach's first mayor after the town was incorporated in 1909, has stood in the median of Royal Palm Way, facing the Royal Park Bridge, since 1947.

Between 1914 and 1923 Oscar A. Jose Sr. developed the Poinciana Park subdivision, just north of the Royal Park Addition, comprised of the three **"Sea" Streets:** Sea Breeze, Sea Spray, and Sea View Avenues. (The names were later contracted into a single word.)

With the opening of the Royal Park Bridge in 1911 and Ocean Boulevard in 1916, the automobile finally arrived in Palm Beach.

From Cocoanut Row, turn left (east) on Royal Palm Way and then make the next right (south) on Hibiscus Avenue. Continue 0.4 mile to the end of Hibiscus Avenue and turn right on Worth Avenue. Drive past the Everglades Club at 365 Worth Avenue on the left and Via Mizner and Via Parigi on the right, just before the intersection with Cocoanut Row on the right.

Boom Time

 After World War I, Palm Beach—and all of south Florida—experienced a building boom. Seasonal residents moved out of the grand hotels and built homes and clubs; churches, commercial, and public buildings followed. Virtually all the buildings that give Palm Beach its distinctive style were built during the period between the two wars, but especially during the Roaring Twenties. The great architects of the day—Addison Mizner, Maurice Fatio, Joseph Urban, Marion Sims Wyeth, Howard Major, Gustav Maass, and John Volk—all got their starts during this period.

It all began with the Everglades Club at the western end of Worth Avenue, as described in Chapter 3 with vintage photographs and summarized in the sidebar below.

The Everglades Club, Via Mizner, Via Parigi, and Worth Avenue

In 1917 Paris Singer, the 23rd child of Isaac Merritt Singer, inventor of the Singer sewing machine, purchased the land on the shores of Lake Worth where Alligator Joe had his alligator farm, which was a popular tourist attraction during the Flagler Era. He brought architect Addison Mizner to Palm Beach in January 1918 to design what became the private **Everglades Club**, which opened in January 1919. Singer expanded the club's facilities and added apartments, including a tower for his own residence. Mizner built a new façade along Worth Avenue in 1925. Mizner's distinctive design—called Mediterranean Revival—created the look that was to become most closely associated with Palm Beach.

In 1923 **Worth Avenue**, then a dirt road, was named after General William Jenkins Worth, the last commander of US forces during the Second Seminole War (1835–1842). (The lake had been named after him in 1841.)

In 1924-25 Singer commissioned Mizner to design the first shopping arcades at the western end of Worth Avenue, including **Via Parigi** (which means Paris in Italian) and **Via Mizner**. Mizner lived in the tower and adjoining apartment on Via Mizner, called **Villa Mizner**, and had his studio on the second floor of the building to the east.

The development of Worth Avenue moved east from the Everglades Club and Mizner's arcades. The Hodges Building was built at 300 Worth Avenue in 1927 and had Saks Fifth Avenue as its first tenant for over 50 years. The Greenleaf & Crosby jewelry store at 236 Worth Avenue, with its distinctive black and silver art deco façade, was built in 1932. The Worth Avenue Building was constructed at the northwest corner of Worth Avenue and County Road in 1955. The block between County Road and South Ocean Boulevard only became a retail shopping area with the construction of the Esplanade (now called 150 Worth Avenue) in 1980.

Midtown Palm Beach

 N.B. Worth Avenue and its vias are best visited on foot and are not covered in this driving tour. For a more complete description of Worth Avenue and Midtown Palm Beach with vintage photographs, please refer to the walking tour in Chapter 3.

Continue to drive west on Worth Avenue, which curves right (north) and becomes South Lake Drive, alongside Lake Worth and the Palm Beach Marina.

Just beyond the lagoon on the left you will drive past two of Mizner's earliest commissions: **Casa dei Leoni** (House of Lions) at 450 Worth Avenue (built for Leonard Thomas in 1921) and **Villa des Cygnes** (House of the Swans) at 456 Worth Avenue (built for Barclay Warburton in 1922).

Take the first right onto Peruvian Avenue and drive to Cocoanut Row.

At 417 Peruvian Avenue, note **Major Alley**, a collection of six small Bermuda-style row houses built by Howard Major in 1925 as a reaction against Mizner's Mediterranean Revival style.

Turn left on Cocoanut Row and drive north past the Vineta Hotel at 363 Cocoanut Row. Turn right on Brazilian Avenue and drive past the Brazilian Court Hotel (whose entrance was originally on Brazilian Avenue but was later moved to Australian Avenue) to South County Road.

During the Flagler Era, Palm Beach was firmly centered around the Royal Poinciana Hotel and The Breakers. The only bridge was the Florida East Coast railroad bridge, which led to Main Street (now Royal Poinciana Way), on the north side of the Royal Poinciana Hotel. Other hotels were built in the vicinity, first the Palm Beach Hotel in 1902 (which burned down in 1925), and during the land boom of the 1920s, the Royal Danieli, the new Palm Beach Hotel, the Alba (on the site of the old Palm Beach Hotel), and the Whitehall. (The sites of these hotels will all be seen at the end of the driving tour.)

But things changed with the opening of the Royal Park Addition and the Royal Park Bridge 1 mile south of the FEC railroad bridge.

During the 1920s the center of gravity of Palm Beach permanently shifted south, beginning with the opening of the Everglades Club in 1919. New hotels were built nearby, including the Hotel Billows (1923, now demolished), the Lido-Venice (1926, later known as the Chesterfield, and now the Vineta), the Brazilian Court (1926), and later The Colony (1947). Mansions were built in the Estate Section between Hammon Avenue and the new Bath & Tennis Club, which opened in 1927.

To make the shift south official, the **Town Hall** and the adjacent fire station (both designed by the West Palm Beach architectural firm of Harvey and Clarke) were built in the center of the Royal Park Addition in 1925 (the two buildings were connected in 1967 and the fire station moved to a new building across the street), and the **Memorial Fountain** (designed by Addison Mizner and dedicated to honor Henry Morrison Flagler and Elisha Newton Dimick) was built in front of the fire station in 1930.

Harvey and Clarke also designed many of the commercial buildings located on South County Road in or near Town Hall Square, including the **Palm Way Building** at the southwest corner of Royal Palm Way, the **Daily News Building** at the southwest corner of Brazilian Avenue, and the **Buckley Building** at the northeast corner of Chilean Avenue.

Turn right on South County Road and drive south for around half a mile to Gulfstream Road.

Immediately after turning onto South County Road, note the Daily News Building at the southwest corner of Brazilian Avenue, the Memorial Fountain across the street (which was restored in 2016), and the Town Hall just past Memorial Park.

Continue driving south on County Road past Worth Avenue and The Colony Hotel, on the corner of Hammon Avenue.

The Estate Section

One block past The Colony Hotel, turn left on Gulfstream Road. Turn right almost immediately on Middle Road and drive south around 300 yards to Via Marina.

After his success opening the Everglades Club and building a shopping arcade on Worth Avenue, Paris Singer tried his hand at residential development. First, he subdivided land on **Golfview Road**, on the north side of the Everglades Club golf course (now a private road). Then he built the **Singer Addition** nearby on what is now **Middle Road** (originally named **Singer Way**), one of the first subdivisions in what is now called the **Estate Section** of Palm Beach, between Hammon Avenue and the Bath & Tennis Club. Many of the houses on Golfview Road and Middle Road were designed by the architect Marion Sims Wyeth, who designed more than 100 houses in Palm Beach between 1920 and 1973. At 61 Middle Road is the house (Tre Fontane) that Wyeth built for himself in 1924.

Turn left on Via Marina and drive a short distance to South Ocean Boulevard.

At 550 South Ocean Boulevard, on the south side of Via Marina, is a house designed by Maurice Fatio in 1930; its three-story tower overlooking the ocean is faced with Fatio's trademark coquina stone.

Turn right on South Ocean Boulevard and drive 1 block south, then turn right on El Bravo Way. Continue on El Bravo, crossing South County Road. Turn left on Travers Way. Then turn left on El Brillo Way and continue across South County Road back to South Ocean Boulevard.

Around the same time that Paris Singer developed the Singer Addition, 27 acres of ocean-to-lake property owned by Frank M. and Anna L. Clement were platted by Clement and made into **El Bravo Park**, consisting of 36 lots on El Bravo Way and El Brillo Way—together with El Vedado Road, known as **"the Els."** El Bravo is a rare example of a winding road in Palm Beach. Once again, many houses in this addition were designed by Marion Sims Wyeth. Farther south, the **Jungle Point** subdivision was built where Jungle Road stands today.

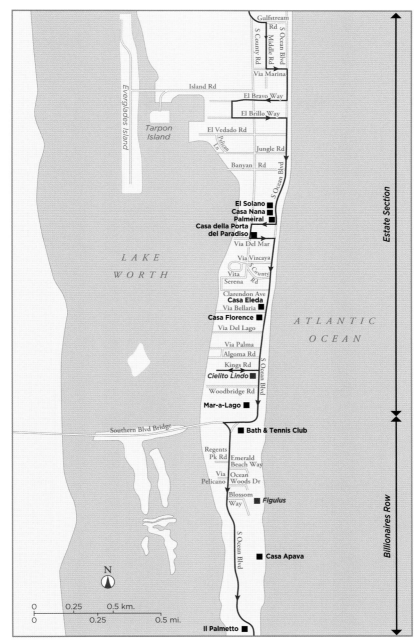

Map of the Estate Section and the northern part of Billionaires Row on the Driving Tour

Noteworthy houses on El Bravo and El Brillo include:

+ 4 El Bravo Way, designed by Marion Sims Wyeth in 1920; Mizner added the tower in 1927.
+ 220 El Bravo Way, **Casa de Miel** (House of Honey), designed by Gustav Maass and John Volk in 1927.
+ 252 El Bravo Way, designed by Volk and Maass in 1928.
+ 343 El Bravo Way, designed by Volk and Maass in 1930.
+ 101 El Brillo Way, **Qui Si Sana** (Here is the Cure), designed by Wyeth in 1921 (on the north corner of El Brillo and South Ocean Boulevard).
+ 640 South Ocean Boulevard, **Villa Tranquilla** (Quiet Villa), designed by Mizner in 1923 (on the south corner of El Brillo Way and South Ocean Boulevard).

Ocean Boulevard in the 1920s

Turn right on South Ocean Boulevard and drive south around half a mile.

In 1916, after four years of construction, **Ocean Boulevard** opened between the Lake Worth (Palm Beach) Inlet and Delray.

Unlike the early settlers, who built on the lake, most of Palm Beach's grandest estates were built on the ocean in the 1920s. Many of them can be seen from Ocean Boulevard.

About half a mile south of El Brillo Way, South Ocean Boulevard jogs slightly west before continuing south. Just after the turn, there are four noteworthy houses in a row:

- 710 South Ocean Boulevard, designed by Mrs. Alfred Kay in the 1920s.

Casa Nana, western elevation, as seen from South County Road

- 720 South Ocean Boulevard, **El Solano**, designed by Mizner in 1919 and once owned by Harold Vanderbilt; purchased by John Lennon and Yoko Ono shortly before Lennon's death in 1980 and owned by Ono between 1981 and 1986.
- 780 South Ocean Boulevard, **Casa Nana**, designed by Mizner in 1926 and first owned by George Rasmussen, who named it after his wife.
- 801 South County Road, **Palmeiral**, designed by Maurice Fatio in 1929 for Margaret Durant Cooper, daughter of General Motors founder William Durant.

Immediately after Palmeiral, turn right on Via Del Selva and drive 1 block to South County Road.

At 115 Via Del Selva is a house designed by Maurice Fatio in 1928. *Turn left on South County Road, and then turn left again at the next street, Via Del Mar.*

Casa della Porta del Paradiso on Via Del Mar

Casa Eleda, as seen from South Ocean Boulevard

At 195 Via Del Mar is **Casa della Porta del Paradiso** (House of the Door to Paradise), which Maurice Fatio considered to be his best work.

At the end of Via Del Mar, turn right back onto South Ocean Boulevard.

Almost immediately on the right are two adjacent houses at 850 and 860 South Ocean Boulevard that were designed by Julius Jacobs in 1928 and 1929, respectively.

Two blocks past the intersection of South Ocean Boulevard and South County Road, two houses designed by Swiss-born architect Maurice Fatio, both built in 1928 with Fatio's trademark exterior of coquina stone quarried in the Florida Keys, straddle Via Bellaria at:

- 920 South Ocean Boulevard, **Casa Eleda** (named after the owner Mortimer Schiff's wife Adele, spelled backward), also known as the "ham and cheese house" because of the distinctive alternating horizontal bands of red brick and coquina stone façade.
- 930 South Ocean Boulevard, **Casa Florence** (built on speculation by Fatio, who first resided there with his wife Eleanor Chase Fatio before selling it to Franklin Simon, a New York City department store owner, in 1932).

Fatio designed seven other houses on Via Bellaria.

Four streets farther south, turn right on Kings Road, drive to the end of the road, and then back to South Ocean Boulevard.

Cielito Lindo, western elevation

In 1927 Marion Sims Wyeth designed 45,000-square-foot, 135-room **Cielito Lindo** (A Little Bit of Heaven) on a 16-acre ocean-to-lake estate for Jessie Woolworth, the daughter of "five-and-ten-cent store" founder F. W. Woolworth, and her husband, James P. Donahue.

In 1947 architect Byron Simonson (who designed The Colony Hotel that same year) saved most of the estate from demolition by dividing it into five smaller but still sizable houses as the Ocean Boulevard Estates. Kings Road now runs through Cielito Lindo's living room.

The 20-room house at 122 Kings Road, the largest remnant of the original mansion, includes Cielito Lindo's entrance hall, tower, master bedroom, and other original rooms. The house across the street at 123 Kings Road includes Cielito Lindo's grand dining room and breakfast nook. Both buildings were designated historic landmarks in 2016.

Once again head south on South Ocean Boulevard.

Immediately on your right, you will pass in front of Mar-a-Lago at 1100 South Ocean Boulevard.

Mar-a-Lago, as seen from Ocean Boulevard

In 1927 Mr. and Mrs. Edward F. Hutton commissioned Marion Sims Wyeth to design **Mar-a-Lago** (Sea to Lake) on 17 acres. Mrs. Hutton (Marjorie Merriweather Post) later hired Joseph Urban to finish the interior and exterior decorations. Upon its completion, Mar-a-Lago was the fifth largest private residence in the United States, with 55,700 square feet and 118 rooms.

In 1973 Marjorie Merriweather Post died and donated Mar-a-Lago to the US government. The federal government returned Mar-a-Lago to her estate in 1980 because it cost too much to maintain.

That same year, Mar-a-Lago was designated a National Historic Landmark and was added to the US Register of Historic Places.

In 1985 Donald Trump purchased Mar-a-Lago and 10 years later he opened the Mar-a-Lago Club.

Of the largest 1920s estates, Mar-a-Lago is the only one to survive with its original property intact.

Just past Mar-a-Lago follow South Ocean Boulevard as it curves west and then turns south once again at the traffic island. Continue south for

Aerial photograph of Mar-a-Lago, looking west

nearly 3 miles to Phipps Ocean Park, where the driving tour ends. (If you wish to shorten your tour, go all the way around the traffic island and head back north on South Ocean Boulevard.) The commentary resumes when you reach Worth Avenue—see "Lido, Rainbo, and Condo" below.)

Billionaires Row

After leaving the traffic island, immediately on your left is the entrance to the **Bath & Tennis Club**, which was designed by Joseph Urban in 1926.

The next 2 miles are along what is now known as "Billionaires Row" since the section includes some of the largest and most magnificent historic (and modern) estates in Palm Beach, including Figulus, Casa Apava, and Il Palmetto.

For the first mile, between the Bath & Tennis Club and Widener's Curve, the estates are directly on the ocean, with South Ocean Boulevard along the lake. For the second mile, between Widener's Curve and Sloan's Curve, today's 16 ocean-to-lake estates are directly on the lake, with South Ocean Boulevard along the ocean.

Around the turn of the 20th century, most of these 2 miles of oceanfront property belonged to two giant estates of 160 acres each known as Figulus, owned by Charles William Bingham, and The

The Bath & Tennis Club, with the tower of Mar-a-Lago above the trees on the right

The Bath & Tennis Club, with Mar-a-Lago at the top right and Bellucia at the bottom left

Wigwam, owned by Richard Croker, which were then gradually subdivided and developed.

In 1881 George Wells Potter (1851–1924) moved to Lake Worth from Miami; he was originally from Ohio. He claimed a homestead on the island that was just south of where the Southern Boulevard Bridge is today and named his property **"Figulus,"** which means potter in Latin.

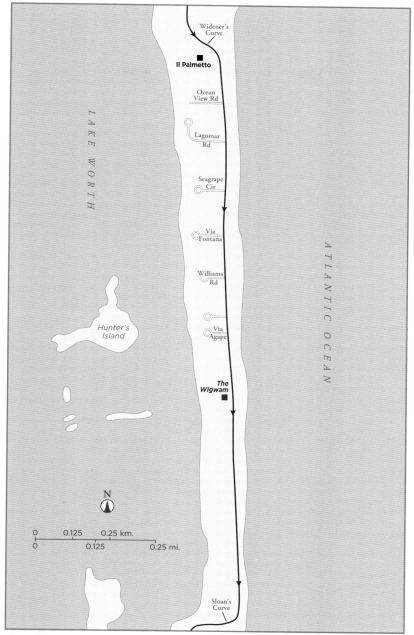

Widener's
Curve

■
Il Palmetto

Ocean
View Rd

Lagomar
Rd

Seagrape
Cir

Via
Fontana

Williams
Rd

Via
Agape

*The
Wigwam* ■

LAKE WORTH

Hunter's
Island

ATLANTIC OCEAN

N

| 0 | 0.125 | 0.25 km. |
| 0 | 0.125 | 0.25 mi. |

Sloan's
Curve

Map of the southern part of the Billionaires Row section of the Driving Tour

The Figulus house was built by the Binghams. Having been damaged in a fire, it was demolished in 1975.

In 1893 Charles William Bingham acquired George Potter's 160-acre Figulus homestead. That same year, he retained master carpenter George Lainhart to build a large Shingle-style house which he named **Figulus**; it was the first privately owned residence built on the ocean in Palm Beach.

Between 1912 and 1916 **Ocean Boulevard** was 50 feet wide and constructed between Lake Worth Inlet and Delray Beach. The new road ran along the ocean bluff for nearly its entire 23-mile length—with the notable exception of the 1-mile stretch through Figulus, where Charles W. Bingham's refusal to grant a right-of-way along the ocean resulted in Ocean Boulevard's being diverted along the lake until it returned to the ocean at what later became known as Widener's Curve.

In 1919 Charles W. Bingham conveyed Figulus and 17 acres to his daughter Elizabeth Bingham Blossom (**"the Blossom Estate"**) and gave an adjacent ocean-to-lake 17-acre parcel to his other daughter, Frances Bingham Payne Bolton (**"the Bolton Estate"**).[1]

---

[1]   In 1942, the Bingham, Bolton, and Blossom families leased the nearby islands in Lake Worth, comprising 22 acres and collectively known as Bingham Islands, to the Audubon Society to preserve them as a wildlife sanctuary. The lease extends to 2041.

Casa Apava, as seen from Lake Worth

Il Palmetto, on Widener's Curve

Aerial photograph of the northern stretch of Billionaires Row above Widener's Curve, March 1927

In 1919 Mrs. Bolton built **Casa Apava**. The architect was J. Abram Garfield of Cleveland, son of President Garfield. Casa Apava, at 1500 South Ocean Boulevard, is still a private residence.

The Binghams sold the land south of the Bolton Estate to developers.

In 1971 Figulus was seriously damaged by fire. The house was demolished in 1975 and the site cleared. In 1979 developer Michael Burrows bought the Figulus estate and subdivided it into 10 lots. Since 2012, more than 20 acres of the original Bingham-Blossom estate have been consolidated into a single estate accessible from Blossom Way (a private road).

In 1930 Maurice Fatio built the 60,000-square-foot, ocean-to-lake estate **Il Palmetto** for Joseph Widener. It is located at 1500 South Ocean Boulevard at what came to be known as **Widener's Curve**.

Follow South Ocean Boulevard as it curves east back to the ocean and continue south along the ocean, past other ocean-to-lake estates, to the next curve west to the lake, known as Sloan's Curve. Continue south on A1A around half a mile to Phipps Ocean Park. Turn left into the parking lot and stop.

The 1-mile stretch of land between Widener's Curve and Sloan's Curve was purchased around 1900 by Richard Croker, who was boss of New York City's Tammany Hall between 1886 and 1902. After his first wife died in 1914, Croker promptly married Beulah Edmondson, a descendant of a Cherokee Indian chief and 50 years his junior, and built a house on his Palm Beach estate nicknamed **"The Wigwam."**

Around 1920, the Crokers sold parcels of their estate to developers. Croker died in 1922. After 20 years of litigation with real estate agents and developers, Beulah Croker declared bankruptcy in 1943 and The Wigwam estate was sold. The house was demolished in 1948, and the property subdivided.

South End

Until the hurricanes of September 17 and October 15, 1947, South Ocean Boulevard continued along the ocean all the way to Delray Beach and beyond. The two hurricanes caused the worst flooding on record in South Florida, covering three million acres from Kissimmee to Florida Bay for 6 months, and destroyed 6 miles of Ocean Boulevard

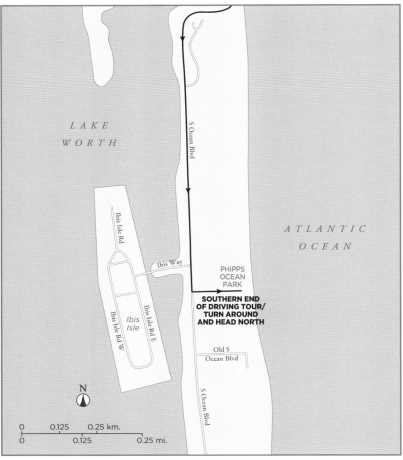

Map of the South End Section of the Driving Tour

The Ambassador Hotel before the 1947 hurricanes

between Sloan's Curve in Palm Beach and Chillingworth Curve in Manalapan. The entire stretch was permanently shut down and A1A (as Florida's east coast road had been renamed in 1946) was rerouted alongside Lake Worth. The **Ambassador Hotel**, which was one of the first buildings constructed in the South End of Palm Beach and had just opened at 2780 South Ocean Boulevard, suddenly found itself directly on the beach.

First apartment buildings and then condominium buildings were soon constructed on the previously vacant—now oceanfront—property. The 4-mile stretch of road south of Sloan's Curve leading to the southern border of Palm Beach at the Town of South Palm Beach

Ocean Boulevard before the 1947 hurricanes, with the future Phipps Ocean Park in the center opposite the future Ibis Isle, with the Ambassador Hotel and Lake Worth Bridge in the distance, and the future Sloan's Curve at the bottom right corner now includes more than 50 condominium buildings and is known as **"Condo Row."**

Sloan's Curve is named after Alfred P. Sloan, who was head of General Motors from 1923 to 1956. In 1941 he purchased a house at 1960 South Ocean Boulevard that had been built by architect Maurice Fatio in 1935. Sloan's house was immediately north of the curve created when the new road was built along the lake following the 1947 hurricanes. Sloan's house was demolished in 1988 and replaced with a new mansion.

In 1948 the Phipps family donated 1,200 feet of oceanfront property for use as a public park, now named **Phipps Ocean Park**, where the **Little Red Schoolhouse** stands. It was built in 1886 and was the first schoolhouse in southeast Florida. It was originally located on Lake Trail about a mile north of today's Flagler Memorial Bridge. The Little Red Schoolhouse was relocated to Phipps Ocean Park in 1960 and restored in 1990.

Heading north on Ocean Boulevard in the 1920s

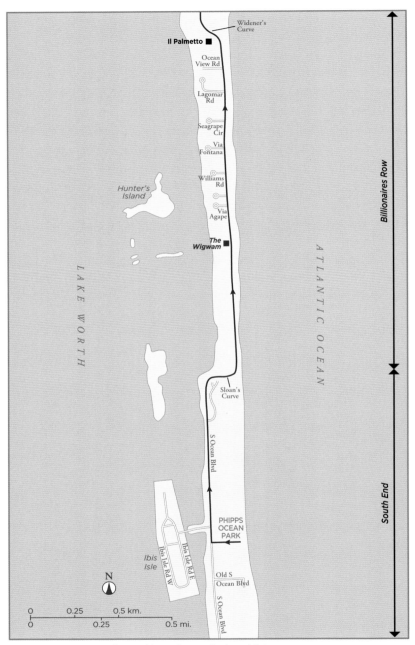

Widener's
Curve

Il Palmetto ■

Ocean
View Rd

Lagomar
Rd

Seagrape
Cir

Via
Fontana

Williams
Rd

Via
Agape

Hunter's
Island

The
Wigwam ■

L A K E
W O R T H

A T L A N T I C   O C E A N

Sloan's
Curve

S Ocean Blvd

PHIPPS
OCEAN
PARK

*Ibis
Isle*

Ibis Isle Rd E

Ibis Isle Rd W

Old S
Ocean Blvd

S Ocean Blvd

N

| 0 | 0.25 | 0.5 km. |
| 0 | 0.25 | 0.5 mi. |

Maps of return route from Phipps Ocean Park to Midtown

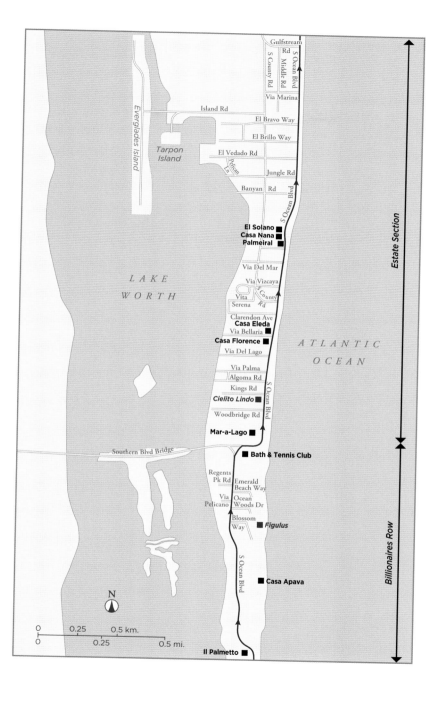

Gulfstream
Rd
S Ocean Blvd
Middle Rd
S County Rd

Via Marina

Island Rd

El Bravo Way

El Brillo Way

El Vedado Rd

Pelican Ln

Jungle Rd

Tarpon
Island

Banyan   Rd

S Ocean Blvd

EVERGLADES ISLAND

■ El Solano
■ Casa Nana
■ Palmeiral

L A K E
W O R T H

Via Del Mar

Via Vizcaya
S County Rd
Vita
Serena

Clarendon Ave
■ Casa Eleda
Via Bellaria
■ Casa Florence

Via Del Lago

A T L A N T I C
O C E A N

Via Palma
Algoma Rd
Kings Rd
■ Cielito Lindo

Woodbridge Rd

■ Mar-a-Lago

Southern Blvd Bridge

■ Bath & Tennis Club

Regents
Pk Rd
Emerald
Beach Way
Via
Pelicano
Ocean
Woods Dr
Blossom
Way   ■ Figulus

S Ocean Blvd

■ Casa Apava

N

Estate Section

Billionaires Row

0   0.25   0.5 km.
0   0.25   0.5 mi.

■ Il Palmetto

Across the South Ocean Boulevard from Phipps Ocean Park is **Ibis Isle**, which was developed by the Phipps family's Bessemer Properties in 1953.

The Town of Palm Beach extends a further 3.5 miles south to its border with the Town of South Palm Beach. This stretch includes the Palm Beach Par-3 Golf Course (built by Michael Phipps in 1961, acquired by the Town of Palm Beach in 1973, redesigned in 2009) and the Lake Worth Beach Casino (first built in 1922, rebuilt in 1947, renovated in 2013) and pier (the original wooden fishing pier opened in 1960, the new concrete pier opened in 2009), but mostly condominiums built in the 1970s and 1980s. So, our driving tour will turn around at Phipps Ocean Park and head north from here.

Leave Phipps Ocean Park and drive back north on South Ocean Boulevard for approximately 5 miles, to Royal Palm Way.

Lido, Rainbo, Condo

Around 4.5 miles to the north, note the **clock tower** on the east side of the intersection of South Ocean Boulevard and Worth Avenue. This marks the former location of the 1,000-foot-long **Rainbo Pier**, built by Gus Jordahn in 1924; it was demolished in 1969. On the southwest corner of Worth Avenue and South Ocean Boulevard, Jordahn had built the **"Welcome to Our Ocean"** pool in 1914. In the 1920s he enlarged the facility and changed the name to **Gus' Baths**. New owners renamed it **Lido Pools** in 1931. The bathhouse and pools were demolished in 1970, and the Winthrop House condominium was built on the site.

Lido Pools with Rainbo Pier at upper left

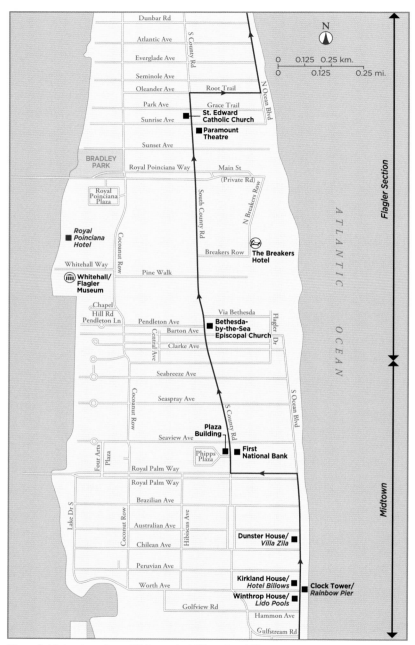

Map of driving tour from Midtown to Millionaires Mile

The next half-mile between Worth Avenue and Royal Palm Way is lined with condominiums built during the 1960s and 1970s, including the following buildings (from south to north):

- **Winthrop House**, 100 Worth Avenue, built by developer Michael Burrows in 1970 on the former site of **Lido Pools**.
- **Kirkland House**, 101 Worth Avenue, built by Michael Burrows in 1974 on the former site of the **Hotel Billows**, which had opened in 1923.
- **The 400 Building**, 400 South Ocean Boulevard, designed by Edward Durrell Stone in 1963.
- **Dunster House**, 360 South Ocean Boulevard, built by Michael Burrows in 1978 on the site of the **Villa Zila**, a house built in 1914 in the Prairie Modern style associated with Frank Lloyd Wright that was later converted into the Shorewinds Motor Hotel.
- **Lowell House**, 340 South Ocean Boulevard, built by Michael Burrows in 1975.
- 300 South Ocean Boulevard, designed by Howard Chilton in 1960.
- 100 Royal Palm Way, designed by Howard Chilton in 1969 and built on the former site of **La Fontana**, a mansion designed by Mizner for George Luke Mesker in 1923.

Turn left on Royal Palm Way.

Halfway down the block on the right, at 151 Royal Palm Way, you will pass a yellow building with the name of the Gunster law firm on the front. This is the last remaining single-family house (now used as an office building) on Royal Palm Way. After the new Royal Park Addition opened in 1911, Royal Palm Way was lined with houses, including the residence of Elisha Dimick. Only when the zoning was changed from predominantly residential to commercial in 1973 were office buildings constructed, which resulted in the "Bankers Row" that it is today.

At the first stoplight on Royal Palm Way, turn right on South County Road and drive north for approximately 1 mile, past Royal Poinciana Way, to Root Trail on the right, which is 1 block past Green's Pharmacy and St. Edward Catholic Church.

Landmarks from the 1920s

On the northeast corner of South County Road and Royal Palm Way stands the **First National Bank Building** (now occupied by Wells Fargo). Maurice Fatio designed the first building on the site in 1925. Marion Sims Wyeth designed the original First National Bank Building in 1927. John Volk designed the neoclassical addition on the north side of the building in 1937 and replaced Wyeth's Moorish façade with another neoclassical temple front in 1955. (John Volk was the most prolific architect in Palm Beach, completing over 1,000 commissions between his arrival in Palm Beach in 1925 and his death in 1984.) The entire group of six buildings between Royal Palm Way and Seaview Avenue was renovated in 2017.

Across South County Road is **Phipps Plaza**. In 1924 the Phipps family's Palm Beach Company commissioned Addison Mizner to design the **Plaza Building** on South County Road. The Plaza Building,

The First National Bank Building, 1940

264 South County Road (1930) on the left, and the Plaza Building (1924) on the right, straddling the entrance to Phipps Plaza

where shops like Bonwit Teller and Brooks Brothers were located, became the anchor for Phipps Plaza, a combination of residential and commercial buildings constructed around an oblong green space.

In 1930 Mizner designed the 2-story quarried-keystone office building on the south side of the entrance to Phipps Plaza, at **264 South County Road**, for the brokerage firm E.F. Hutton. It was one of his last commissions. Since 2022 it and the adjacent building at 270 South County Road, which was designed by Maurice Fatio, house the Carriage House club.

A half-mile farther north on the right, you will pass the third **Bethesda-by-the-Sea Episcopal Church**, which was built in 1927; it was designed by the New York firm of Hiss and Weeks. The Cluett Memorial Gardens behind the church were dedicated in 1931.

Drive past The Breakers and the former US Post Office at the top of Royal Poinciana Way (built in 1937). The next two streets are Sunset Avenue and Sunrise Avenue.

During the construction of the Royal Poinciana Hotel, Black workers, including many from Caribbean islands and former slaves from southern states, formed a settlement called **the Styx**, centered around today's Sunset and Sunrise Avenues. In 1910 the residents of the Styx relocated to two all-Black neighborhoods in West Palm Beach, and the

The third Bethesda-by-the-Sea Episcopal Church

The Paramount Theatre with The Breakers in the distance

St. Edward Catholic Church

site was developed as the **Floral Park Addition** by brothers Edward R. and John R. Bradley; it was one of Palm Beach's first two subdivisions, along with the Royal Park Addition.

At the southeast corner of Sunrise Avenue and North County Road is the **Paramount Theatre**, which was designed by Joseph Urban in 1927. The Paramount, with its 1,236-seat auditorium, presented movies as well as live performances. (The theater closed in 1980 and the auditorium was converted into offices.)

On the northwest corner of Sunrise Avenue is **St. Edward Catholic Church**, which was built in 1926. It was designed by Mortimer Dickerson Metcalfe. Edward R. Bradley was the single largest contributor to its construction.

Two streets farther north, turn right on Root Trail and follow it to the end, at the ocean.

Root Trail in the 1890s

Wells Road was originally lined with 136 Australian pines that were planted in the 1920s.

Root Trail, named after Enoch Root, who first owned the land, is lined on the north side by modest bungalows built mostly in the early 1900s that were occupied by employees of the two Flagler hotels. Originally a sand road, Root Trail, with its small wood-frame houses, is the only street in town that still gives a sense of what Palm Beach must have looked like at the turn of the 20th century, outside the grand hotels, none of which has survived.

Turn left on North Ocean Boulevard and follow it 5 blocks to the end. Then turn left on Wells Road and continue until the stop sign, where it intersects with North County Road. Turn right and follow North County Road and then North Ocean Boulevard all the way to the Lake Worth Inlet, a distance of 3.4 miles.

Millionaires Mile

When Ocean Boulevard opened between Lake Worth (sometimes known as Palm Beach) Inlet and Delray Beach in 1916 after four years of construction, it ran along the ocean bluff for its entire 23-mile length, except for the half-mile stretch between Figulus and Widener's Curve, where it ran along the lake. The half-mile between Wells Road and Country Club Road became known as the first "Millionaires Mile" (although it could now be called Billionaires Row North), following the construction of some of Palm Beach's grandest ocean-to-lake estates in the 1910s and 1920s. Many of the estates were built on the 1,000 feet of oceanfront north of Wells Road purchased in 1912 by Henry S. Phipps (1839–1930), who made his fortune as Andrew Carnegie's partner in U.S. Steel. Phipps subdivided the land into three parcels where his sons Henry Carnegie and John S. "Jay" and daughter Amy built houses and sold some of the land to brothers Charles and Gurnee Munn who also built houses.

Ocean Boulevard after the 1928 hurricane

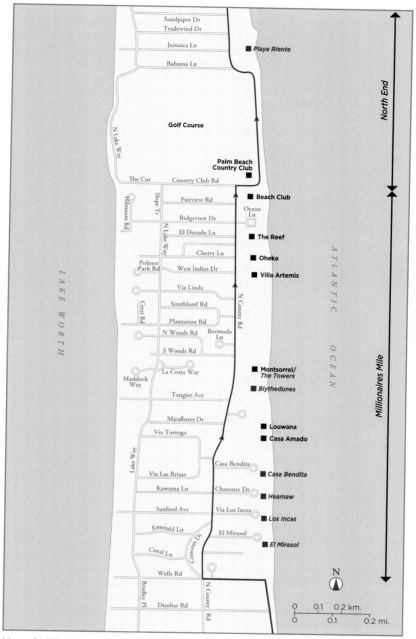

Sandpiper Dr
Tradewind Dr
Jamaica Ln
Bahama Ln

■ *Playa Riente*

Golf Course

N Lake Way

Palm Beach
Country Club
■

The Cut   Country Club Rd

■ **Beach Club**

Slope Tr
Fairview Rd

Hillmount Rd
Ridgeview Dr

Ocean
Ln
□

El Dorado Ln

■ **The Reef**

N Lake Way

Cherry Ln

■ **Oheka**

Polmer
Park Rd
West Indies Dr

■ **Villa Artemis**

Via Linda

Crest Rd
Southland Rd

Plantation Rd

N Woods Rd   Bermuda
Ln

N County Rd

S Woods Rd

Maddock
Way
La Costa Way

■ **Montsorrel/**
The Towers

Tangier Ave

■ *Blythedunes*

Miraflores Dr

■ **Louwana**

Via Tortuga

■ **Casa Amado**

Lake Way

Casa Bendita

■ *Casa Bendita*

Via Las Brisas

Kawama Ln   Chateaux Dr

■ *Heamaw*

Sanford Ave   Via Los Incas

■ *Los Incas*

Emerald Ln

Crescent Dr
El Mirasol

■ *El Mirasol*

Coral Ln

Wells Rd

Bradley Pl
Dunbar Rd
N County
Rd

LAKE WORTH

ATLANTIC OCEAN

Millionaires Mile

N

0   0.1   0.2 km.
0   0.1   0.2 mi.

Map of Millionaires Mile section of Driving Tour

From left to right: Heamaw, Casa Bendita, Amado, Louwana, Blythedunes, and The Towers estates—all directly on the ocean, so after the 1928 Hurricane. Los Incas is below Heamaw. Villa Artemis is beyond The Towers.
Credit: Courtesy DeGolyer Library, Southern Methodist University.
Photograph by Robert Yarnall Richie (1908–1984), circa 1932–1934.
Part of Robert Yarnell Richie photograph collection.

From their construction until the 1928 hurricane, Ocean Boulevard separated these great estates from the beach. After the hurricane destroyed the road, the landowners in this section successfully petitioned the town to abandon this stretch of Ocean Boulevard, and instead to extend County Road (formerly known as Palm Beach Avenue) north from Wells Road to the Palm Beach Country Club. The estates then moved their entrances to County Road, where they were given the street addresses that are referred to below.

From south to north, the first great estates built on the ocean on **Millionaires Mile**, and their fates, were as follows:

Heamaw was designed in 1916 by Francis Burrall Hoffman Jr., the architect of James Deering's estate Vizcaya in Miami, for Henry Carnegie Phipps. Heamaw was razed in 1972 after the death of his widow, Gladys Mills Phipps.

El Mirasol, 1932

Los Incas was built on 6 acres around 1916 for Michael P. Grace, John S. Phipps's father-in-law, by an unknown architect. It was demolished in 1978 and subdivided; it is now the site of Via Los Incas.

El Mirasol (the Sunflower), 348 North County Road, was Addison Mizner's first Palm Beach mansion following the construction of the Everglades Club with its distinctive Mediterranean Revival design. The oceanfront estate was built on 42 acres stretching between the Atlantic Ocean and Lake Worth in 1919 for Edward and Eva Stotesbury. After the 1928 hurricane, its entrance was moved from Ocean Boulevard to County Road. In the 1930s Maurice Fatio designed a grand new entrance portal for El Mirasol, now at 365 North County Road between today's streets El Mirasol and Via Los Incas. In 1958 El Mirasol was razed. In 1964 Robert Gottfried developed 12 oceanfront acres as El Mirasol Estates. The name of the street El Mirasol and Maurice Fatio's portal are all that remains of the estate today.

Casa Bendita, western elevation

Casa Bendita was built by Addison Mizner on 28 acres for John S. "Jay" Phipps and his wife Margarita "Dita" Grace, after whom the house was named. In 1961 Casa Bendita was demolished and the land east of County Road was turned into a 12-lot subdivision. In 1993 14 acres of the 20-acre parcel on the west side of County Road was platted as the Phipps Estates subdivision. The name of the street Casa Bendita is all that remains of the original estate.

Casa Amado and **Louwana**, which share a driveway at 455 North County Road, were designed by Mizner in 1919 for brothers Charles and Gurnee Munn. Louwana was named after Gurnee's wife, Mary Louise Wanamaker. Both houses are still private residences.

Blythedunes, 515 North County Road, was designed by Harold Hastings Mundy for Robert Dun Douglass in 1915. The house was demolished in 1985 and the land was subdivided.

The Towers, 548 North County Road, was designed by Mizner in 1923 for William M. Wood. Two towers, one five stories high, gave

The Towers was demolished in 1965.

the house its name. The Towers was razed in 1965 and **Montsorrel** (Mountain of Sorrow) was built in its place in 1969. Montsorrel was designed by French architect Jacques Regnault. The guest house across North County Road was built around 1990. The two properties total 13 acres.

Villa Artemis, 656 North County Road, was designed in 1916 by Francis Burrall Hoffman Jr. for Henry S. Phipps's daughter Amy Phipps Guest (Mrs. Frederick Guest). In 1967, new owners removed the second story of the house and fundamentally changed the original design of the house. Villa Artemis is still a private residence.

Oheka, 691 North County Road, was designed by Maurice Fatio in 1930 for banker Otto Hermann Kahn. (The name was derived from the first letter of his first name and the second letters of his middle and last names.) After Kahn's death, the estate was sold to the Graham-Eckes School, which occupied the premises between 1941 and 1989. The school then sold the house to an individual owner who converted the building into a private residence once again.

Oheka

The Reef

The Reef, 702 North County Road, was designed by Maurice Fatio in 1935, when tastes turned against building large mansions in favor of smaller, more livable houses. It is one of the few houses in Palm Beach designed in the International Style. It is still a private residence.

More Clubs

At 755 North County Road is the **Beach Club**, which was built in 1970 on the former site of the **Coral Beach Club**, which opened in 1947 and was owned by Jack Mitchell until his death in 1969. Jack was famous for his colorful attire, wide-brimmed straw hats, and pink Cadillac convertible. Both clubs were designed by John Volk.

The Coral Beach Club was built by Jack Mitchell in 1947.

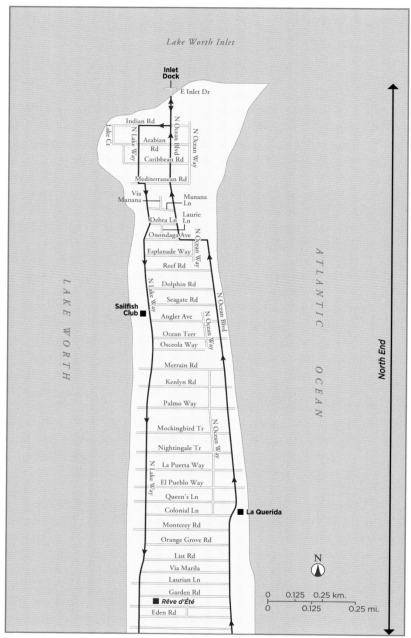

Map of the North End section of the Driving Tour

The first Palm Beach Country Club opened in 1917 on the newly built Ocean Boulevard.

Immediately after the Beach Club, follow the road as it curves east to the ocean. Continue north along the ocean for approximately a quarter-mile; then follow the road as it curves back inland before heading north once again. (If you wish to shorten the tour, turn left just past the Beach Club onto Country Club Road. Then turn left again at the next corner, where there is a stop sign, just before entering The Cut, onto Slope Trail, which becomes North Lake Way, and drive south.) The commentary resumes at "Return Leg from Pioneer Era to Flagler Era to Boom Time to Today"—see below.

Immediately on your left on the ocean is the **Palm Beach Country Club** at 760 North Ocean Boulevard. In 1917 the East Coast Hotel Company (owner of the Royal Poinciana Hotel and The Breakers) opened the Palm Beach Country Club, the town's second golf course, on the highest and hilliest part of the island, on the advice of its designer Donald Ross. The land previously belonged to the **Florida**

The new Palm Beach Country Club opened in 1953. The clubhouse is in the center on the ocean, overlooking the golf course. To its right on the ocean is the Coral Beach Club.

Gun Club, which was a popular destination for hotel guests during the Flagler Era.

In 1952 the Palm Beach Country Club was sold to an investment group which built a new clubhouse and reopened to new membership in 1953.

More Mansions

Just past the Palm Beach Country Club and the curve away from the ocean, at 947 North Ocean Boulevard, once stood **Playa Riente** (Laughing Beach), built by Mizner in 1923 for Oklahoma oilman Joshua Cosden and later owned by Anna Thompson Dodge. With 70 rooms built on 27 acres of ocean-to-lake property, Playa Riente was Mizner's largest and most elaborately decorated residence in Palm Beach. The house was demolished, and the land was subdivided in 1957.

Playa Riente, western elevation

Playa Riente, eastern elevation, with the Palm Beach Country Club's golf course on the left

Soon on the left you will drive past Eden and Garden Roads; in the middle of the island they are linked by Adam Road.

In 1887 Charles and Frances Cragin of Philadelphia purchased 20 acres where they built their home **Rêve d'Été** (Summer Dream). They soon added 15 more acres and planted an exotic botanical garden known as the "Garden of Eden," which became a popular destination for guests at the Royal Poinciana Hotel and The Breakers. The property was sold in 1925. In the 1930s, it was subdivided into Garden, Eden, and Adam Roads.

At 1095 North Ocean Boulevard, Mizner designed **La Querida** (Dear One) for Rodman Wanamaker II, who sold it to Joseph P. Kennedy in 1933. After an already extensive restoration of La Querida by the previous owner in 2017, the new owners started an even more ambitious expansion in 2022. All that remains of the original structure are the wall and door along North Ocean Boulevard.

Rêve d'Été with a corner of its famous cactus garden, which featured 500 varieties of cactus, on the left

La Querida, which served as the Winter White House during John F. Kennedy's presidency

End of the Road

*Stop at the Lake Worth Inlet at the end of North Ocean Bou-
levard. There is no place to park, but passengers should take
the opportunity to get out and walk to the end of the dock and
admire the view of the inlet, Singer Island on the other side,
and Peanut Island to the left, while the driver waits in the car
in case a bus comes along.*

In 1918 the new **Lake Worth Inlet (sometimes known as the
Palm Beach Inlet)** opened, separating Palm Beach from Singer Island
(which Paris Singer started to develop in 1925, before falling victim to
the Florida real estate bust of 1927). The jetties were added in 1935,

The Lake Worth Inlet (at bottom) was first dredged in 1918. The jetties were
added later. The old natural inlet is above.

The Lake Worth Inlet dock at the northern tip of Palm Beach in the 1950s

and the channel has been enlarged and deepened three times. Dredging the inlet led to the creation of Inlet Island as a "spoil site," which grew every time the inlet was dredged; it started at 10 acres and is now up to 84 acres. Inlet Island was renamed **Peanut Island** after it was leased for use as a peanut oil–shipping terminal, which failed in 1946.

A wooden dock once stood at the north end of Palm Beach at Lake Worth Inlet. Between 1946 and 1985 it was known as **"Annie's Dock"** after Anne Eggleston, who was the dock master and lived in a tiny house on the dock. The dock had a fuel pump and a bait shop. It was replaced by today's concrete dock.

The north end of Palm Beach in 1950

Turn around and head south. Turn right at the first street, Indian Road. Then turn left on the next street, North Lake Way. Follow North Lake Way for 4.4 miles until it becomes Bradley Place and then, on the far side of Royal Poinciana Way, Cocoanut Row, to the Henry Morrison Flagler Museum, where the driving tour ends.

Return Leg from the Pioneer Era to the Flagler Era to Boom Time to Today

When you reach the Palm Beach Country Club's golf course, this was where early settler Harlan Page Dye opened the 63-room **Hotel Lake Worth** in 1888. It was the largest hotel on Lake Worth until Henry Flagler built the Royal Poinciana Hotel. The hotel burned down in 1897.

At the end of the golf course, follow the road east through "The Cut."

The original, narrow Coral Cut

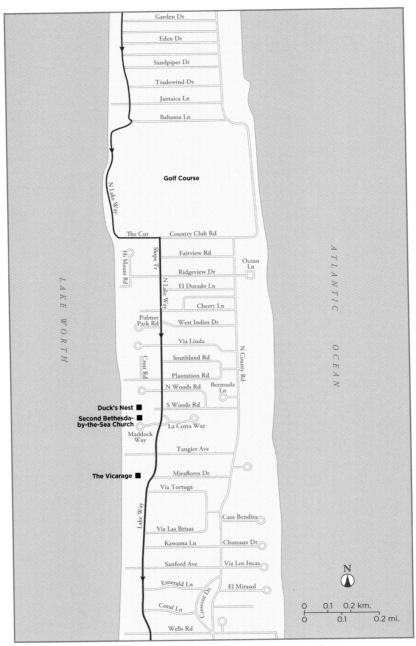

Map of the Lake Way to Cocoanut Row section of the Driving Tour

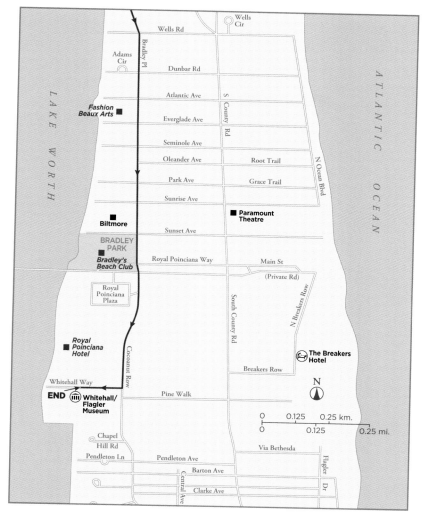

In the 1920s the **Coral Cut, also known as The Cut,** was excavated to provide additional access to the North End of the island. It was later widened.

At the first stop sign, turn right on Slope Trail, which becomes the continuation of North Lake Way.

N.B. For vintage photographs of the buildings on Lake Trail from south to north, as summarized in the sidebar below, please refer to the walking and biking tour in Chapter 1.

Early Structures on Lake Trail

Around 1 mile south on your right is Maddock Way, where the second Bethesda-by-the-Sea Church, constructed on the lake in 1895, and the adjacent house to the north, Duck's Nest, built in 1891, are located. The church was deconsecrated when the current Bethesda-by-the-Sea Church was built in 1927 and is now a private residence. Duck's Nest has been enlarged over the years.

The Vicarage, 448 North Lake Way, was built in 1897 to house Bethesda-by-the-Sea's vicar/rector. It is the third oldest house in Palm Beach.

Farther south, after North Lake Way becomes Bradley Place, on the right side is the Villa Plati townhouse subdivision at 230 South Bradley Place, between Atlantic and Everglade Avenues. The townhouses were built in 1991-92 on the former site of the **Royal Danieli**

The Fashion Beaux Arts Building in the front center was built on the lake between Everglade and Seminole Avenues in 1917 and demolished in 1965.

Hotel, which opened in 1924, was renamed the **Hotel Mayflower** in 1930, and became the **Palm Beach Spa** in the 1960s.

On the next block south are the L'Ermitage condominiums at 200 South Bradley Place, between Everglade and Seminole Avenues. They were built in 1985 on the former site of the **Fashion Beaux Arts Building**, which was designed by August Geiger in 1917 and was Palm Beach's first stand-alone entertainment and shopping center, with a cinema and retail stores. The Fashion Beaux Arts Building was converted into an apartment building in 1944 and demolished in 1965.

Two blocks farther south is the Palm Beach Biltmore Condominium building. The 12-story building was originally the **Alba Hotel**, which opened in 1926 on the former site of the 400-room Palm Beach Hotel, which was built in 1902 and burned down in 1925 when high winds blew embers from the second Breakers fire, located half a mile away, onto its roof. The Alba became the Ambassador Hotel in 1929 and the **Biltmore Hotel** in 1934. The building was converted to condominiums (with 128 units) in 1981.

On the left, at the corner of Bradley Place and Sunset Avenue, is the **White Elephant Hotel**. Originally named the **Algomac Hotel**, then the **Bradley House Hotel** until 2020, it was built by Edward R. Bradley, owner of Bradley's Beach Club, in 1926.

The Alba Hotel on Lake Worth was later renamed the Biltmore Hotel.

Changes to Flagler Era Palm Beach
1934–1958

In 1938 the first **Flagler Memorial Bridge** replaced the original Florida East Coast Railway Bridge; a landscaped median replaced the train station; a second, eastbound street replaced the railroad tracks; and Main Street and the new street were renamed **Royal Poinciana Way** (even though the way was lined with royal palm trees).

The new Flagler Memorial Bridge leading to the south side of the new Royal Poinciana Way, where train tracks were originally laid. Main Street is on the north side of the median strip, where the train station once stood.

Royal Poinciana Way in the 1940s with the water tower still in the median

Royal Poinciana Way with the water tower removed, circa 1960s

The Beach Club and E. R. Bradley's adjacent residence in the foreground, with the north façade of the north wing of the Royal Poinciana Hotel above and to the left (before its demolition in 1935), and the 10-story tower of the Whitehall Hotel (built in 1927) on the lake above and to the right. This photograph was taken before 1938, when the FEC railroad bridge was replaced by the Flagler Memorial Bridge.

On the right just before the bridge is **Bradley Park**. Bradley's Beach Club closed after 48 years in 1945 and Edward R. Bradley died the following year. His wife having predeceased him and being childless, Bradley willed the 4.5 acres of land where both his casino and adjacent house stood to the Town of Palm Beach for a public park. A wall and pagoda-style mantel and fireplace from his house were saved and are now located at the north side of the park, where they are known as the Bradley Pavilion. The park was enlarged and improved in 2017 following the construction of the latest Flagler Memorial Bridge, which opened in 2017.

Drive across Royal Poinciana Way, continuing south on Cocoanut Row to the Flagler Museum, on Whitehall Way, where this driving tour ends.

The **Royal Poinciana Hotel**, which occupied nearly the entire space between the Flagler Memorial Bridge and Whitehall, was demolished

Bradley Park with fountain looking up Royal Poinciana Way

In 1934-35 the Royal Poinciana Hotel was demolished; only the Slat House was spared. It is now an office building on Cocoanut Row just south of Royal Poinciana Plaza.

in 1934-35, 40 years after it was built; only the **Slat House**, which was built after the 1928 hurricane, and the adjacent giant Mysore fig tree were spared. With its enormous, exposed roots and 150-foot branch spread, the Mysore fig tree (sometimes called a banyan or ficus tree) at the southern edge of the parking lot of the Royal Poinciana Plaza is the largest of its kind in Palm Beach.

The empty lots to the right (south) of the new Flagler Memorial Bridge are where the Royal Poinciana Hotel stood for 40 years. The lighter-colored rectangular lot on the left will be the site for the Royal Poinciana Plaza. The larger lot with two white areas on the right will be occupied by the Palm Beach Towers apartment building. To the left (north) of the new Royal Poinciana Way, the new Bradley Park stands where E. R. Bradley's Beach Club once stood, next to the Biltmore Hotel.

After the Royal Poinciana Hotel was demolished, **Cocoanut Row** was extended to connect Royal Palm Way with Royal Poinciana Way.

In 1950 the Phipps family's Bessemer Properties acquired the Royal Poinciana property west of Cocoanut Row from the Florida East Coast Hotel Company for commercial development. Bessemer sold the southern portion of the property to developers who built the **Palm Beach Towers** at 44 Cocoanut Row in 1956.

In 1958 Bessemer built the Regency-style **Royal Poinciana Plaza** shopping center and the 900-seat **Royal Poinciana Playhouse** on the 12 acres to the north; both were designed by John Volk. Royal Poinciana Plaza was renovated with new landscaping in 2016. The Royal Poinciana Playhouse was rebuilt starting in 2023 and is expected to reopen in 2025.

The Palm Beach Towers under construction

Royal Poinciana Plaza with the Royal Poinciana Playhouse on the lake

Flagler's Legacy

 Flagler died in Palm Beach in 1913. His third wife and widow, Mary Lily Kenan Flagler Bingham, remarried in 1916 and died in 1917. She left Whitehall to her niece, Louise Clisby Wise Lewis, who in 1924 sold Whitehall to new owners who converted it into a hotel. In 1926 they added an 10-story, 250-room tower behind the original building. In 1959 Flagler's granddaughter Jean Flagler Matthews bought the **Whitehall Hotel**, tore down the tower, and restored the mansion to its former glory. The **Henry Morrison Flagler Museum** opened in 1960. It was a fitting tribute to the man whose impact on the Town of Palm Beach and the State of Florida is without equal.

The Whitehall Hotel with its 10-story tower behind Henry M. Flagler's original residence

The Henry Morrison Flagler Museum, restored to its original splendor, opened in 1960.

Selected Bibliography

Curl, Donald W. *Mizner's Florida—American Resort Architecture*. The Architectural History Foundation and the Massachusetts Institute of Technology, 1984.

Curl, Donald W. *Palm Beach County—An Illustrated History*. Windsor Publications, 1986.

Drake, Lynn Lasseter, and Richard A. Marconi, with the Historical Society of Palm Beach County. *Images of America—West Palm Beach 1893 to 1950*. Arcadia Publishing, 2006.

Gillis, Susan, Richard A. Marconi, and Debi Murray. *Images of America—Palm Beach County During World War II*. Arcadia Publishing, 2015.

Historical Society of Palm Beach County. *Palm Beach County History Online*. www.pbchistoryonline.org.

Historical Society of Palm Beach County with Russell Kelley. *An Illustrated History of Palm Beach—How Palm Beach Evolved Over 150 Years from Wilderness to Wonderland*. Pineapple Press, 2020.

Hoffstot, Barbara D. *Landmark Architecture of Palm Beach*. Rowman & Littlefield, Fourth Edition, 2019.

Marconi, Richard A., and the Historical Society of Palm Beach County. *Then and Now—Palm Beach*. Arcadia Publishing, 2013.

Marconi, Richard A., and Debi Murray, with the Historical Society of Palm Beach County. *Images of America—Palm Beach*. Arcadia Publishing, 2009.

Mayhew, Augustus. *Lost in Wonderland—Reflections on Palm Beach*. Palm Beach Editorial Services, 2012.

Mayhew, Augustus. *Palm Beach—A Greater Grandeur*. East Side Press, 2016.

Mayhew, Augustus. Various articles in the online *Palm Beach Social Diary*.

The *Palm Beach Post* and the Historical Society of Palm Beach County. *Palm Beach County at 100—Our History, Our Home*. The *Palm Beach Post*, 2009.

About the Authors

The Historical Society of Palm Beach County—The Historical Society of Palm Beach County, a nonprofit organization, was formed in 1937 with the mission to collect, preserve, and share the rich history and cultural heritage of Palm Beach County. The HSPBC maintains a large archive on the history of Palm Beach County, Florida, and the Caribbean, which includes four million photographic images, plus maps, newspapers, journals, periodicals, architectural drawings, and research files. The creation of the Richard and Pat Johnson Palm Beach County History Museum in 2008 finally allowed the collection to fully serve its critical purpose: to share and showcase the rich history of Palm Beach County and the larger context of Florida's heritage dating back at least 12,000 years. In addition, the multiple education programs and initiatives of the Society in schools and communities are of primary importance to our vision of building an understanding and appreciation of local history in our children.

Russell Kelley—Born in Palm Beach, Russell Kelley returned to his hometown after a career abroad. The changes in Palm Beach ignited his desire to learn how his hometown evolved from the sleepy town of his youth into the sophisticated resort of today. This curiosity led to his research with the Historical Society of Palm Beach County resulting first in *An Illustrated History of Palm Beach*, and now in *Historic Palm Beach: Walking, Biking, and Driving Tours.*